UNCIVIL WAR

UNCIVIL WAR

RACE, CIVIL RIGHTS & THE NATION.

Introduction by Derrick Bell

Editor/ Eyal Press
Series Editor/ Peter Rothberg

THE NATION PRESS.

CONTENTS

CHAPTER III.
Profiles of Hope and Rage

CHAPTER IV.
Voices

ACKNOWLEDGEMENTS

We wish to thank Veronica Stephens for her exemplary research and illuminating opinions. We also owe debts of gratitude to Deborah Thomas for her ideas, enthusiasm and creative talents; Katrina vanden Heuvel for her encouragement and support; Richard Lingeman for his help with headings; JoAnn Wypijewski for her editorial advice; Tom Gogola for the title; Teresa Stack for her publishing expertise; Jennifer Miller for her photo research; and Neil Black and Victor Navasky for believing in this book and our ability to produce it. Finally, special thanks are due to Emily Gordon for copy-editing the entire contents in very short order. This book was much improved by her expert work.

— *Eyal Press and Peter Rothberg*

EDITOR'S NOTE

This anthology does not pretend to include all of the best writing on race and civil rights that has appeared in *The Nation* in the past 130 years. It features, instead, selections that illuminate the magazine's steadfast commitment to racial justice in a variety of voices and hues. The pieces have been grouped into four separate but overlapping chapters. What unites them is not content or style but a particular manner of engaging with the subject at hand: each is infused with moral passion and a critical edge. Each deals not in the confines of the possible but in what the author thinks and feels is right. Each, finally, engages some aspect of Martin Luther King Jr.'s simple but enduring questions: "Why is equality so assiduously avoided? Why does white America delude itself, and how does it rationalize the evil it retains?"

The writers in this anthology have addressed these questions not to embitter but to provoke, educate, arouse and inspire. It is certainly true, as James Baldwin once wrote, that "the story of the Negro in America is the story of America. . . . It is not a very pretty story." At the same time, Baldwin and others in this collection shed light on the ugliness of American racism to certify that it is intolerable, that America can—must—do better.

While this anthology covers race and racism in its multiple guises, it deals exclusively with black-white relations and not with the experiences of all American ethnic groups. The book, furthermore, necessarily reflects *The Nation*'s past and present composition: more male than female, more white than black and certainly more white male than black female contributors. That said, all of the writers in this volume deal seriously with racial issues, and as a group represent a wide range of political and personal points of view.

For reasons of space, some articles have been edited. But the original language is unaltered. It is both more honest and more edifying, I believe, to retain words like "negro" and other terms of the day. If these words offend, that is all the more reason to remember where, how and by whom they have been used.

—*Eyal Press*
New York City
April 1995

Introduction

The Nation's editors—from its abolitionist founders to the present—have provided space for those persistent and too often lonely voices inveighing against the evils of racial injustice. It is, thus, appropriate that the editors are launching their new series of books with this collection of articles from past issues reviewing the illogic of a racism that persists and even flourishes despite the inequity of its product: stable profits and undeserved power for the few, and political and economic subordination for most Americans—white as well as black.

The many manifestations of racism described in these essays—the horror of death by lynching, the soul-wrenching humiliation of segregation, the irrational resistance to even those social reforms sought by blacks that are as badly needed by whites—all serve a dual function. They focus public attention on a racial policy or practice that commands attention, sparks debate, and attracts hordes of supporters and opponents who wage ideological battle in the legislative chambers, the courts, the media, and—on occasion—in the streets. More importantly, fiery racial confrontations deflect attention from the major motivation for racial division, a division that W.E.B. Du Bois articulated 70 years ago in a description that is hardly less accurate today. By deliberately encouraging race hatred between black and white workers, managers were able to keep both submerged and hard at work in the post–World War I South. This hostility was manipulated to prevent the two groups from uniting and emancipating themselves from those who exploited both.

Du Bois then poses the question at the heart of the race issue that—as he predicted—bedeviled this country during the twentieth century, and threatens its destruction in the twenty-first:

> What induces white labor to place so low a value on its own freedom and true well-being and so high a value on race hatred? . . . The Southern white laborer gets low wages measured in food, clothes, shelter and the education of his children. But in one respect he gets

high pay and that is in the shape of the subtlest form of human flattery—social superiority over masses of other human beings. Georgia bribes its white labor by giving it public badges of superiority. The Jim Crow legislation was . . . to flatter white labor to accept public testimony of its superiority instead of higher wages and social legislation.

Segregation, as Du Bois knew, represented an update of the "we whites must stand together against them" preaching by slave owners that led working-class whites to accept and even defend a system of human bondage, their allegiance to which condemned them to marginal status in an economy where only the rich could afford slaves. Today, the miracles of technology are enabling major companies to export whole plants to third-world countries, while casting off millions of American workers. In the name of efficiency and in the quest for profits, scores of proud, middle-income employees are being transformed into fearful, part-time expendables laboring away with low pay, no benefits, and no job security.

All too many whites, though, mesmerized by the still-workable formula, readily attribute the loss of their jobs or anxiety about their future to affirmative action or some other policy they are told—and readily believe—is intended to provide unearned benefits to unworthy blacks. As a result, racial hostility is increasing as income levels and opportunities decrease for whites as well as blacks. Whites deem the dire conditions in so many black communities proof of our unworthiness rather than an all-too-vivid preview of their fate.

It is a source of wonder that, despite consignment to the archetypal, scapegoat role, many blacks have sacrificed much in an effort to make real the nation's professed commitment to freedom and justice for all. They, and those whites from the abolition movement to the present who have stood with them, have seldom won praise during their lifetimes. Rather, as Jesse Jackson put it, "those who have fought for the highest and best principles of our country, the true patriots, have been vilified and crucified [for they] invariably disturb the comfortable and comfort the disturbed, and are persecuted in their lifetimes even as their accomplishments are applauded after their deaths."

Such was the fate of Fannie Lou Hamer, whose insurgent challenge at the 1964 Democratic convention in Atlantic City forced the Democratic Party to declare itself for what it was: an undemocratic party when it came to blacks.

Her conviction helps explain her courage in the face of beatings and death threats. "We're tired of all these beatins'. We're tired of takin' this. It's been a hundred years and we're still being beaten and shot at, crosses are still being burned, because we want to vote. But I'm goin' to stay in Mississippi and if they shoot me down, I'll be buried here."

Mrs. Hamer's readiness to die for freedom is beyond the comprehension of most who hold public office. For them, even the prospect of political martyrdom is anathema. During an unacknowledged era of crisis in which courage of this character is needed more than ever, the seductive blandishments of racial scapegoating easily entice those seeking elective office. To avoid the hard issues, they rely on the rich array of code phrases that translate now as throughout our history: "Keep the nigger down."

Even those unwilling to appeal to the public's base instincts hope to effect social reforms through leadership by consensus. Martin Luther King Jr. warned that no major social reforms can be achieved in this way. The issues are too momentous, the contest too heated. "The search for a consensus will tend to become a quest for the least common denominator of change. In an atmosphere devoid of urgency the American people can easily be stupefied into accepting slow reform, which in practice would be inadequate reform."

This insistence to concede nothing to injustice is echoed throughout this book. From William Pickens's appraisal of Jim Crow Texas in 1923 to Barbara Deming's report from the Birmingham Jail in 1963, to Andrew Kopkind's look at media coverage of the Jesse Jackson campaign in 1983, it is clear that real, lasting change can only come out of urgency and persistence.

Racism as a social stabilizer has always been immoral and has become essential to the society's survival. The danger, though, has been present from the beginning. There is some reassurance in the fact, amply illustrated in the pages of *The Nation*'s new book, that there are always those willing to speak the truth about race and racism. It is a message as urgently needed as it has been, up until now, mostly ignored.

—Derrick Bell
Scholar in Residence,
New York University Law School
April 1995

Chapter One

~

THE WOUNDS OF HISTORY:
RACE, VIOLENCE & JUSTICE

"Go Right Ahead!"

December 13, 1933 by W. Steig

~1866~

The Moral of the Memphis Riots
E.L. Godkin

E.L. Godkin co-founded *The Nation* and served as editor from 1865 to 1899.

MAY 15, 1866 ~ There was one feature of the late riot at Memphis which is worthy of attention from its bearings upon the political status of the negroes. It appears by the more recent and trustworthy accounts of the affair that it began in an unsuccessful attempt made by the police to put a stop to the disorderly conduct of some negro soldiers. The row which followed was taken up by the citizens at large, and when renewed in the afternoon, after a short pause, it took the form of a general massacre of such of the colored population as showed themselves in the streets. This part of the tragedy appears to have been inconceivably brutal, but its brutality was, after all, not the most remarkable thing about it. Its most novel and most striking incident was, that the *police* headed the butchery, and roved round the town either in company with the white mob or singly, and occupied themselves in shooting down every colored person, of whatever sex, of whom they got a glimpse. In the half-organized attack made on the fort, also, the police were the principal assailants.

We are not going to furbish this occurrence up into any argument for the wholesale disenfranchisement of the South, or for any greater severities against her white population than we are now inflicting upon them. Anybody who expects Southern whites and blacks to settle down into their true and just relations to each other without breaking one another's heads a good deal knows little either of history or human nature. There will prevail in the South for a long time to come a good deal of envy, hatred, and malice towards the colored population, and they will show themselves in riots and outrages more or less flagrant. What was peculiar about the Memphis riot was that the officers of the law, the very persons on whom the colored population will have to rely for protection as soon as the troops are withdrawn, took a leading part in it, and we now have very little doubt that, were any similar outburst of popular prejudice to take place tomorrow in any other town in the South, the local police, if they interfered at all, would interfere in the same way. "They would stand by their race," as Mr. James T. Brady once said, in a speech before the war, when Northern Democrats were trembling lest the Southern blacks should break loose, come North, and eat them all up. The negro would, when pursued by a mob, avoid "the guardians of the public peace" as vigilantly as he would any of the pack at his heels. We grant that under the State law and under the Federal law he would have his remedy against all his assailants. He could sue them either civilly or criminally, or both, for assault and battery, or assault and false imprisonment, or for a felonious assault. If his house was burnt or his furniture damaged by a popular rising, he could sue the county for damages. He might get a verdict, and he might not. We will suppose that he would; but which of us would live in any community where this was our main reliance for protection against mob violence? Which of us would keep our families in a town in which not only were we objects of popular odium, but in which, if an attempt were made to mob us, we might expect to see the policeman who patrolled our street taking the first pop at us with his revolver, or the sheriff of the county heading a party charged with the duty of ramming in our front door?

When the Freedmen's Bureau bill and the civil rights bill were first talked of, one of the strongest arguments used against them by their opponents was that they were unnecessary, that "the laws of political economy" would eventually secure protection for the negroes from their white neighbors themselves without any interference on the part of the Federal Government. No matter how much their old masters might dislike them, the necessity of employing them, of relying on them for prosperity and comfort, would sooner or later make the relations of the two races, if not cordial, at least amicable. The negro had only to wait a little and all would be right by-and-by. We always thought there was something in this argument, but we nevertheless always considered it a most ridiculous argument when addressed to the blacks themselves. It was substantially this: "Your white neighbors are at present greatly incensed against you. They consider you the cause of all their troubles, and look upon themselves as having been robbed of your services. Therefore, for some time to come, they will probably maltreat you a good deal. They will most likely rob and murder you frequently; and more frequently they will flog you and deny you justice in the courts. Your house will, probably, be burnt now and then, and you will be driven from one part of the country to the other by mobs. But you must not mind this. They will get over their feelings toward you after a while, and get used to seeing you free, and then they will most likely let you alone, or at least not annoy you so much. The laws of political economy are all working for you, and you know whenever you want to travel abroad you can have a United States passport. In the meantime pay your taxes regularly, and put your trust in Providence. The Federal Government can do nothing else for you." The negro might very naturally reply that he cared nothing for the laws of political economy; that what he wanted was the protection of the Government to which he paid his taxes and owed his allegiance; that very likely the whites would get used to him after a while and let him alone, and, whenever that time came, of course he would not need any protection. But that it is precisely at those periods of a man's life when his neighbors don't like him, and want to attack him, that governments and police are needed, and that for any government to announce that it could do nothing at these crises was to destroy its sole claim on his fidelity.

~ 1919 ~
Protecting Southern Womanhood

From the 1860s to the 1940s, *The Nation* published numerous reports on lynching and mob violence. Herbert J. Seligmann, the author of several books on race and ethnography, was among those who inveighed against the brutal rituals of the post–Civil War South.

Herbert J. Seligmann

JUNE 14, 1919 ~ A revealing chapter of American history is yet to be written on the methods employed to "protect Southern womanhood." Those methods have included in the past two months an orgy of men and women about a dying human being whose legs slowly burned as a rope strangled him and fifty bullets entered his body; they have included the murder of innocent men without trial; they have included the invasion of a hospital by a mob, resulting in the death of a patient just operated upon; they have included the forcible removal from a railway car and the murder of an innocent man whose leg had just been amputated in the hospital from which he was being transported. For the benefit of those unfamiliar with the increasingly popular sport of "protecting Southern womanhood" it should be noted that the objects of this sport are usually United States citizens of dark skin—Negroes.

We learn from the editorial page of the *Vicksburg Weekly Herald* of May 16 that the sport in Vicksburg, where it claimed an innocent victim nineteen years old, was stimulated by a country-wide campaign for equal rights for United States citizens (Negro). We learn that published reports of that campaign acted "like oil on fire" in Vicksburg, where a human being (Negro) was roasted amid "the fiendish gloating" of a mob, to quote a local newspaper, of 1,500 persons, some of the spectators being women (white). We learn from the columns of the *New Orleans Times-Picayune* of May 12 that the sport received a special impetus in the case of a Negro artisan who was so skilled in his occupation that he competed successfully with white men who resented his success. From a study of authenticated cases it would seem that where there is a white man to be shielded from the consequences of wrongdoing, where a Negro is a rival in trade or business of white men, where a Negro attempts to change his status from that of laborer to property owner and farmer, or where a Negro falls under suspicion of attempting to exercise the functions of a citizen guaranteed him by the Federal Constitution, there stares him in the face the danger that he will be done to death in any one of a number of hideous ways by a mob of white men intent upon "protecting Southern womanhood."

George Bolden (Negro) was accused of "writing an insulting note to a white woman" in the town of Monroe, Louisiana. Responsible citizens of the town testified that he could not write and that he had had to make a "cross mark" when he endorsed checks payable by them to him. Nevertheless a mob shot him and left him for dead. He was carried to the hospital, where his leg was amputated in consequence of the injuries which the mob had inflicted. Learning he was in the hospital, the mob, despite the protest of the nurses, invaded a ward filled with patients, some of whom were critically ill, "one having just undergone an operation." They seized this man (Negro) "but discovered their mistake and left him." He died of shock the following day. Bolden, his leg amputated, was turned over the next day to his wife, who was advised to take him to Shreveport. The mob boarded the train on which he lay in the baggage car. Near Cheniere, eight miles west of Monroe, one of their number pulled the bell cord, stopping the train. "As the train slowed down," says the reporter for the *New Orleans Times-Picayune* of May 12, "the mob rushed into the baggage car and threw the Negro off. . . . Bolden's body literally was riddled with bullets."

And now for the protection of Southern womanhood which occasioned the murder. "Reports are also in circulation," says the *Times-Picayune*, "to the effect that Bolden, who was skilled in certain lines of work, had incurred the enmity of a small coterie of white men who are said to object to Negroes being employed at trades that require skill, and that one of the white men in this coterie wrote the note to the white woman and signed Bolden's name to it."

Southern womanhood was again protected in Vicksburg on May 14. A young white woman of that city, Mattie Hudson, eighteen years old, living on Second North Street, screamed at five o'clock that morning and said she had waked to find a Negro in her bed. The man escaped. At ten o'clock, two bloodhounds from Crystal Springs, Mississippi, were baying down a street inhabited by Negroes. Every Negro man then at home knew that if one of those dogs stopped at his door he would be murdered by a mob without having opportunity to explain. One Negro who watched the dogs from his place of hiding informed the writer that they started toward the steps of a white man's house in First North Street but were pulled back by their owner, Gantt, who held them in long leashes. Lloyd Clay, nineteen years old, was arrested. He had come downstairs to see what caused the disturbance outside his house. His younger brother, aged seventeen, testified that Lloyd had slept in the same room with him the entire night. Lloyd Clay was favorably known. His family had lived in Vicksburg for several generations and bore a good name. "Brought before Miss Hudson, she declared he was not the man who attacked her last night," said the *Vicksburg Evening Post*.

Miss Hudson, being protected, was brought to the corner of Farmer and Clay streets, in Vicksburg's residential district. "Shouts, howls, and the screech of motor horns made a deafening sound. In the midst of this confusion the men brought Clay to Miss Hudson." It will be remembered that she had said he was not the man. But here was a howling mob, thirsting for the blood that would protect Southern womanhood. "Is that the man?" they shouted at Miss Hudson. "Say the word," shouted others. Miss Hudson said the word. The following passages are taken from the first page of the *Vicksburg Evening Post:*

> The mob fell upon the Negro, snatching away his clothes and beating him. He was dragged further toward First North. "Shall we do it?" asked a big man of the crowd. The answer came in long continued cheers of approval. . . . The Negro was hauled up five feet but slipped back. The sight of the nude body rising above the crowd increased the excitement. . . . "Shoot him," someone called. "No, no," came the answer, "let him die slow." The Negro, with head twisted, dangled limply from the line. Seeing that Clay was merely suffering discomfort, men below began to jerk his legs. Others smeared kerosene upon the body, while others prepared a bonfire below, saturating the material with gasoline. . . . The flesh on the body began to crinkle and blister. The face of the Negro became horribly distorted with pain. He assumed an attitude of prayer, raising his hands' palms together. . . . The legs of the corpse curled backward grewsomely. . . . The grizzly form was allowed to dangle for an hour and a half in the moonlight. . . . Men of all classes, women, and even children witnessed the scene. The whole affair had been witnessed by many ladies who followed the mob from the jail and others who joined the crowd on the terraces nearby. . . . When the body fell to the gutter there was a great rush for bits of rope as souvenirs.

Lest there be doubt as to the motive of the mob, I quote the remark of a man made in reply to the request of Mrs. Ida M. Keefe that the tree on which Clay was hung in front of her house be cut down. "Madam," said the man, "the tree is a monument to the spirit of manhood of this community who will not tolerate crimes against their women folks. What was done here last night was done for you and for every woman and girl in Warren County."

From the instances and the figures cited, it would seem that passion is aroused over mob murders, not because they are committed in defense of Southern womanhood, but because the entire relations of white and colored races are involved. In casual conversations in Mississippi Delta cities the following stimulants to mob murder were cited to me: 1. The nation-wide campaign for equal rights for Negroes. 2. Induction of Negroes into the United States Army, "putting them on an equality with white men." Cheap politicians, of whom Senator Vardaman is typical, refer to "French-women-ruined Negro soldiers," using every resource of this kind to foment race hatred, which is their chief stock in trade. 3. Survival of the fear of Negro domination inherited from carpetbagger days. 4. The economic motive in all its variants, based upon the determination to deny the Negro his rights, to "keep the nigger in his place." 5. The sport in torture: Page 1 of the *Vicksburg Evening Post*, recounting the murder of Clay, had this passage: "'Have you had enough fun, boys?' a leader asked. 'Yes, cut him down.'"

Unfortunately, racial animosity is exhibited not only in lynchings. Race riots are constantly threatened. Not one Negro to whom I spoke in the Delta region but wished to get away. Daily life for them is almost intolerable. Negroes are subject to every insult and abuse, not to mention Jim-Crowism, and they have had too much experience of the courts to rely on them. It is not surprising that they have purchased arms in a number of Southern cities with the intention of defending their lives and the lives of their families if conflict is provoked.

~ 1931 ~

Eight Who Must Not Die
Dorothy Van Doren

During the 1930s *The Nation* published several articles in defense of the Scottsboro Boys—nine blacks who in 1931 were convicted of raping two white girls on flimsy evidence. The novelist Dorothy Van Doren was the first to contest the verdict in the magazine's pages.

June 3, 1931 ~ On March 24 last seven young white men and two girls dressed in men's overalls hopped a slow freight moving south along the Memphis and Charlotte Railroad in northern Alabama. Already on the freight were a crowd of young Negro boys—some stories say as many as nineteen or twenty, not riding together but distributed along the various cars of the train. A couple of men along the way as the train passed saw that a fight was going on between Negroes and whites. Since they were some distance away they could not distinguish the faces of the boys and were not able, of course, to identify them later. But in the course of the fight the white men were thrown off the train, all but one who landed between two cars and was dragged back to safety by one of the Negroes. The men who were thrown off were not too much injured to rush to the nearest station at Steventon, tell their story to the telegraph operator, and have a wire sent to the train a station or two up ahead. By the time the train reached Paint Rock, Alabama, it was met by the sheriff and his deputies, all the Negroes who were on board—twelve by now—were taken off, the two girls in overalls were likewise removed, and the whole party was taken to the Scottsboro jail.

At this point the stories of the affair begin to differ. One account declares that the girls were in a fainting condition, sobbing, speechless, having evidently been subjected to some horrible experience. Another describes them as quite calm and not disposed to make any charges against the Negro boys until after they had conferred with the white officials and learned that young ladies who ride unchaperoned with Negro youths in freight cars must of necessity consider themselves raped, and raped they thereupon decided they had been. Whatever the truth, the girls were examined shortly after they left the train by two physicians in Scottsboro, who found them in good physical condition, not bruised, not fainting, not, apparently, seriously affected by whatever experience they had passed through. There were evidences of sexual intercourse but indications that it had taken place some hours before. They were mill girls, one a little over twenty, one a little under; the older one had been divorced.

The girls declared that their clothes had been torn from their bodies, that they had been attacked each by six Negroes, that all of them were armed with knives except two who had guns, that the assaults were actually perpetrated while their assailants had weapons in their hands. It was evident that feeling against the Negroes, never deeply sleeping, was thoroughly and dangerously aroused.

On March 30 a grand jury returned indictments for rape against the nine boys. Rape in Alabama is punishable with death, although the extreme penalty is invoked rarely, and then against Negroes charged with rape of white women. A week later, April 6, was the date set for the trial, it being also the day for horse-swapping in the community, when large crowds would naturally assemble at Scottsboro courthouse.

Two of the boys were tried separately ahead of the rest. They were the oldest of the lot, one of them having actually attained to the ripe age of twenty. The trial took a day, the jury was out an hour and a half. A crowd of 10,000 persons—which in a little town of something over a thousand inhabitants is quite a crowd—was milling around the courthouse, waiting to hear the verdict. When the jury returned, a great hush descended over the mass of waiting people—mostly men, for women and children had by order of the judge been excluded from the courtroom. The *Chattanooga Times* is eloquent:

> Thunderous applause late this afternoon greeted a Jackson County grand [*sic*] jury's verdict of guilty for Charlie Weems and Clarence Norris, Negro hobos, who were convicted of attacking a white girl. . . . Hardly had the echoes of the trial died away until the trial of Haywood Patterson, Chattanooga Negro, charged with the same offense, was resumed.

The *Times* might have added that a brass band, mysteriously evoked from nowhere, entertained the uproarious multitude with the "Star Spangled Banner" and "Dixie" immediately after the verdict was announced.

The rest of the trial proceeded in due course. Eight of the boys were found guilty and sentenced to die in the electric chair. The ninth, a lad of fourteen, was too young for the death sentence. The state asked for life imprisonment. But seven of the jurors held out for death anyway, and the judge declared a mistrial. Only Victoria Price was willing to identify the defendants. Ruby Bates, the other girl, confessed that she could not do so. No other identification was made. Mrs. Price's testimony was conflicting throughout. Yet she was positive that the nine very black youths whom, presumably, she had never set eyes on before, were the ones out of the crowd on the train who had attacked her and her companion, although of course she was almost beside herself while she was trying vainly to defend her person from them.

On the whole the boys told a straightforward story. They had been on the train. Some of them had not even been in the freight car in which the fracas took place. Some of them had taken part in it—one of them, the youngest, Roy Wright, was the one who had reached out a hand and kept the white youth from falling beneath the cars. They had done nothing to the girls. Because they had not, they had not thought it necessary to leave the train as half a dozen Negroes did, though they, too, had ample opportunity to do so before it was stopped. The fact that they did not leave the train affords, on the whole, the strongest presumption of their innocence. For why a Negro, even a Negro of low intelligence as these boys evidently are, who has committed an attack on a white woman should remain at the scene of his crime when he has opportunity to leave it is a question that no rational person can answer.

The point that should be at issue is that eight boys, black or white, seven of them under twenty years of age, should not die for a crime that they did not commit, and if they did not commit a crime, should receive the benefit of every legal safeguard to protect their rights and their lives.

The two girls were casuals, young women whose reputation is, to put it mildly, not of the best. Efforts of the defense attorney to discredit them at the trial were mostly circumvented, but enough was read into the record to make their testimony dubious. They are locally well known as prostitutes, supplementing their miserable wages as mill workers by the only other occupation they know. The nine Negro boys are likewise casuals. None of them can read or write. All have unsavory reputations. They have been accused of various petty crimes—gambling, thieving, more or less harmful mischief in general. They are not noble characters: it is a safe guess that not one of them will ever amount to much. They are the products of ignorance, of the most wretched and extreme poverty, of dirt, disorder, and race oppression. Yet there is no reason in the world why they should not have every legal right accorded to the finest and most cultivated person in the land. They are poor and ignorant and irresponsible. All the more should the state protect them, all the more should every device of the courts and every safeguard of the law be invoked to the end that justice be served.

~ 1 9 5 5 ~

Justice in Sumner:
Land of the Free . . .

Dan Wakefield

In the summer of 1955, Dan Wakefield visited *The Nation*'s offices and offered to cover the Emmett Till murder case in Mississippi if the magazine would buy him a bus ticket to Sumner. The report he sent back was his first article to be published in a national magazine.

Sumner, Mississippi

OCTOBER 1, 1955 ~The crowds are gone and this Delta town is back to its silent, solid life that is based on cotton and the proposition that a whole race of men was created to pick it. Citizens who drink from the "Whites Only" fountain in the courthouse breathe much easier now that the two fair-skinned half brothers, ages twenty-four and thirty-six, have been acquitted of the murder of a fourteen-year-old Negro boy. The streets are quiet, Chicago is once more a mythical name, and everyone here "knows his place."

When the people first heard that there was national, even worldwide publicity coming to Sumner and the murder trial they wondered why the incident had caused such a stir. At the lunch recess on the first day of the trial a county health-office worker who had stopped by to watch the excitement asked a visiting reporter where he was from, and shook his head when the answer was New York City.

"New York, Chicago, everywhere," he said. "I never heard of making such a mountain of a molehill."

The feeling that it all was a plot against the South was the most accepted explanation, and when Roy Bryant and J. W. Milam ambled into court September 19 they were armed not only with their wives, baby boys, and cigars, but the challenge of Delta whites to the interference of the outside world. The issue for the local public was not that a visiting Negro boy named Emmett Louis Till had been dragged from his bed and identified later as a body that was pulled from the Tallahatchie River with a seventy-pound cotton-gin fan tied around its neck with barbed wire—that issue was lost when people learned that the world was clamoring to have something done about it. The question of "nigger-killing" was coupled with the threat to the racial traditions of the South, and storekeepers set out jars on their counters for contributions to aid the defense of the accused murderers.

Donations to the fund disqualified several prospective jurors, as prosecutors Gerald Chatham, district attorney, and Robert B. Smith, special assistant attorney general appointed to the case, probed carefully at every candidate for a day and a half before accepting the jury. Judge Curtis Swango, a tall, quietly commanding man, combined order with a maximum of freedom in the court, and when he had Cokes brought in for the jury it seemed as appropriate courtroom procedure as pounding the gavel.

While the jury selections went on inside, the crowds outside the building grew—and were automatically segregated. Aging, shaggy-cheeked Anglo-Saxons with crumpled straw hats lined a long wooden bench. Negroes gathered across the way at the base of the Confederate statue inscribed to "the cause that never failed." The Negro numbers increased, but not with the Negroes of Sumner. A red-necked deputy whose pearl-handled pistol showed beneath the tail of his sportshirt explained that the "dressed-up" Negroes were strangers. "Ninety-five per cent of them's not ours," he said. "Ours is out picking cotton and tending to their own business."

Moses Wright, a Negro locally known as a good man who tends to his business, was the state's first witness. He pressed his back against the witness chair and spoke out loud and clear as he told about the night two white men came to his house and asked for "the boy from Chicago—the one that did the talking at Money"; and how the big, balding man came in with a pistol and a flashlight and left with Emmett Till. Mose fumbled several times under cross-examination but he never lost his straightforward attitude or lowered his head. He still of course was "old man Mose" and "Uncle Mose" to both defense and prosecution, but none of that detracted from the dignity of how he told his story.

The rest of the week he was seen around the courthouse lawn with his pink-banded hat tilted back on his head, his blue pants pulled up high on a clean white shirt by yellow-and-brown suspenders. He walked through the Negro section of the lawn with his hands in his pockets and his chin held up with the air of a man who has done what there was to do and could never be touched by doubt that he should have done anything less than that.

When Mose Wright's niece, Mrs. Mamie Bradley, took the stand it was obvious as soon as she answered a question that she didn't fit the minstrel-show stereotype that most of Mississippi's white folks cherish. Nevertheless, the lawyers of both sides were careful to always address her as "Mamie," which was probably wise for the favor of the jury, since a

Clarksdale, Mississippi, radio station referred to her as "Mrs. Bradley" on a news broadcast and spent the next hour answering calls of protest.

J. J. "Si" Breland, dean of the defense attorneys, questioned her while he remained in his seat, occasionally slicing his hands through the air in the quick, rigid motions he moved with throughout the trial. She answered intelligently, steadily, slightly turning her head to one side as she listened to questions, replying with a slow, distinct emphasis. "Beyond the shadow of a doubt," she said, "that was my boy's body."

At lunchtime recess the crowds around the soft-drink and sandwich concession debated her identification of her son, and many were relieved in the afternoon session when Tallahatchie County Sheriff H. C. Strider squeezed his 270 pounds in the witness chair and said the only thing he could tell about the body that had come from the river was that it was human.

Sheriff Strider, who owns 1,500 acres of cotton land, farms it with thirty-five Negro families, has the grocery store and filling station on it, and operates a cotton-dusting concern with three airplanes, is split in his commitments in a way that might qualify him as the Charles E. Wilson of Tallahatchie County. What's good for his feudal plantation is good for the county, and his dual role as law-enforcement officer and witness for the defense evidently didn't seem contradictory to him. His commitments were clear enough that prosecution lawyers once sent two state policemen to search a county jail for one Leroy "Too Tight" Collins, a key witness for the prosecution who was missing (and never found).

There were still missing witnesses, dark, whispered rumors of fleeing men who saw the crime committed, when Gerald Chatham tugged the sleeves of his shirt and walked over to the jury Friday morning to make the summation of the case for the prosecution. Both he and Smith, who is a former F.B.I. man, had followed every lead and sent state policemen driving through the countryside in search of the Mississippi witnesses, but only two of the four who were named—Willie Reed and Mandy Brandley—were found. The time had come for Chatham to work with what he had.

In a matter of minutes from the time he started talking the atmosphere of the court was charged with tension as he raised his arm toward the ceiling and shouted that "the first words offered in testimony here were dripping with the blood of Emmett Till." The green plaster walls of the room had grown darker from the clouds of the rain that was coming outside, as Chatham went on with the tones, the gestures, the conviction of an evangelist, asserting that "the guilty flee where no man pursueth," and retelling the story of the boy's abduction in the dark of night.

J.W. Milam, the bald, strapping man who leaned forward in his seat during most of the sessions with his mouth twisted in the start of a smile, was looking at a newspaper.

Roy Bryant lit a cigar. With his eyebrows raised and his head tilted back he might have been a star college fullback smoking in front of the coach during season and asking with his eyes "So what?"

When Chatham was finished, C. Sidney Carlton, the able attorney for the defense whose large, fleshy face was usually close to where the cameras were clicking, poured a paper cup of water from the green pitcher on the judge's desk, and opened his summation. He spoke well, as usual, but after Chatham's oratory he was doomed to anticlimax. There had been a brief rain and the sun was out with more heat than ever. Defense attorney J.W. Kellum, speaking briefly after Carlton before the noon recess, had the odds of discomfort against his chances of stirring the jury, but he did his best with the warning that the jurors' forefathers would turn in their graves at a guilty verdict. And then he asked what was undoubtedly the question of the week. If Roy and J.W. are convicted of murder, he said, "where under the shining sun is the land of the free and the home of the brave?"

The question was a fitting prelude to the harangue of John Whitten, the defense's last speaker. The clean-shaven, pale young man in a neatly pressed suit and white shirt that defied perspiration announced his faith that "every last Anglo-Saxon one of you men in this jury has the courage to set these men free."

Mr. Whitten went on to declare he had an answer for the state's most convincing evidence—the ring of Emmett Till that was found on the body discovered in the Tallahatchie River. The body really wasn't Emmett Till, Whitten said, and the ring might have possibly been planted on it by the agents of a sinister group that is trying to destroy the social order of the South and "widen the gap which has appeared between the white and colored people in the United States."

He didn't name any group, but the fondly nurtured local rumor that the whole Till affair was a plot on the part of the N.A.A.C.P. made naming unnecessary.

It took the twelve jurors an hour and seven minutes to return the verdict that would evidently help close the gap between the white and colored races in the land of the free and the home of the brave. Tradition, honor, God, and country were preserved in a package deal with the lives of Roy Bryant and J.W. Milam.

Reporters climbed tables and chairs to get a glimpse of the acquitted defendants, and the newspaper, magazine and television cameras were aimed at the smiles of their wives and families in a flashing, buzzing finale. Then the agents of the outside world disappeared in a rush to make their deadlines and the stale, cluttered courtroom was finally empty of everything but mashed-out cigarettes, crushed paper cups, and a few of the canvas spectator chairs that the American Legion had sold across the street for two dollars each.

The trial week won't be forgotten here soon, and glimpses of the "foreign" Negroes who don't till cottonfields but hold positions as lawyers, doctors, and Congressmen have surely left a deep and uncomfortable mark on the whites of the Delta. But at least for the present, life is *good* again. Funds are being raised for separate-and-equal school facilities in Tallahatchie County and on Wednesdays at lunchtime four of the five defense attorneys join with the other Rotarians of Sumner in a club song about the glad day "when men are one."

~1963~

In the Birmingham Jail

Barbara Deming

Barbara Deming, a writer and civil rights activist, was the only white person arrested in the May 1963 Birmingham demonstrations. She refused to accept bail (which was immediately offered to her) until her fellow demonstrators were freed.

Birmingham, Ala.

MAY 25, 1963 ~ The day I went to jail in Birmingham for joining a group of Negro demonstrators—children, most of them—who were petitioning, "without a license," for the right to be treated like human beings ("that's what it boils down to, that's all we ask"), I experienced more sharply than I ever had before the tragic nature of segregation, that breakdown of communication between human and human which segregation means and is.

The steps which took me from the Negro church in which I spent the early part of that day, May 6, sitting among the children as they were carefully briefed and finally, in small groups, one after another, marched, holding hands and singing, into the streets—"marching toward freedom land"— the steps which placed me swiftly then in the white women's ward of the city jail provided a jolt for the mind that can still, recalling it, astonish me.

The comedian Dick Gregory describes his experience of a similar shock the day he arrived here to join the struggle—describes alighting from the plane and buying a newspaper. Not a word on the front page of the events that were shaking all of Birmingham. He had been afraid for a moment that the plane had put him down in the wrong city. Locked in my jail cell, surrounded by new companions now, I too could ask myself: Am I in the right city? The events of the day were acknowledged as news here; the presence of hundreds of children crowding the cells below us was the chief topic of the white women; but the break with reality was quite as abrupt as though no word about them had been spoken.

The children were no longer children now, the frail boys and girls I had seen singing and clapping their hands and sometimes dancing for a moment in the aisles of the church to find their courage—the amazing courage to walk out and face fire hoses, police dogs, jail sentences; these were now "juveniles"—a word spoken in horror, as though their youth made them particularly dangerous and untrustworthy. These were "niggers" now. "Shit, goddam, they must be fighting among themselves already!" "That's right!" "Goddam, you know it!" "Niggers are wild animals!" "You know it!" "Yes!" "That's right!" "Better keep the door here locked tight." The voices would rise in a frenzied chorus—statement and refrain: then hush in awe; then, a little later, break out again. One prisoner would hurry in from her post at a particular window in an adjoining cell, from which a bit of the front yard could be glimpsed, and report that she had seen police dogs out there. Perhaps they would all be safe, then, against these devils in the same building. "All you have to say to one of them dogs is 'Git'm!' Just: 'Git'm!'" But perhaps even the dogs were not protection enough. "They ought to throw a bomb in there and blow them all up," one woman cried in torment.

Now and then, when the wind was right, I could hear the children's voices from their cells, high and clear—"Ain't gonna let nobody turn me round, turn me round, turn me round. . . . Woke up this morning with my mind set on freedom!"—the singing bold and joyful still; and with that sound I was blessedly in their real presence again. I strained to hear it, to bolster my own courage. For now I was a devil too, of course—I was a "nigger lover." The warden had introduced me to my cell mates, in shrill outrage, and encouraged them to "cut me down" as they chose. They soon informed me that one of the guards had recommended that they beat me up. No one had moved to do it yet, but the glances of some of them were fierce enough to promise it. "What have you got against Southern people?"

The unreal drama continued throughout the six days I remained in jail. Three times a day we left our cell block to go downstairs for meals, shepherded by the warden. Occasionally, on these trips, a group of the Negro children would have to pass us in the halls. "Huddle back there in the corner!" the warden would cry out to us sharply—"up against the wall!" The women would cower back like schoolgirls, while the terrifying people God had cursed—as the warden regularly informed us—filed past, harmless, and some of them even still joyful.

As the days passed, I stopped fearing my cell mates and made friends with them. After a little while this wasn't hard to do. Every women in there was sick and in trouble. I had only to express the simplest human sympathy, which it would have been difficult not to feel, to establish the beginning of a friendly bond. Most of the women had been jailed for drunkenness, disorderly conduct or prostitution. That is to say, they had been jailed because they were poor and had been drunk or disorderly or had prostituted themselves.

One day, in jest, one of the women cried to the rest of us when the jail authorities had kept her waiting endlessly before allowing her the phone call that was her due: "I ought to march with the Freedom Riders!" I thought to myself: You are grasping at the truth in this jest. Toward the end of my stay I began to be able to speak such thoughts aloud to a few of them—to tell them that they did, in truth, belong out in the streets with the Negroes, petitioning those in power for the right to be treated like human beings. I began to be able to question their wild fears and to report to them the words I had heard spoken by the Negro leaders as they carefully prepared their followers for the demonstrations—words counseling over and over not the vengeance they imagined so feverishly ("They all have knives and guns! You know it!") but forbearance and common sense; not violence but nonviolence; I stressed for them the words of the integration movement's hymn: "Deep in my heart I do believe we shall live in peace some day—black and white together." One after another would listen to me in a strange, hushed astonishment, staring at me, half beginning to believe. By the time I was bailed out with the other demonstrators, on May 11, there was a dream in my head: If the words the Negroes in the nonviolent movement are speaking and are enacting ever begin to reach these others who have yet to know real freedom, what might that movement not become? But I was by then perhaps a little stir crazy.

~ 1975 ~

Philadelphia's Brotherly Death: Gunfights in the Graveyard

J.B. Lieber

J.B. Lieber was studying law at the University of Pennsylvania when he wrote this article.

Philadelphia

JANUARY 18, 1975 ~ One sign of urban failure is the vacant lot, razed and forgotten. Another, more horrifying, is the emergence of homicidal street gangs. Philadelphia may be no more craterized than other cities but its gang problem is unparalleled. In 1973, forty-three died in the guerrilla fighting, the highest figure in the country, and the 1974 toll promises to be of the same order. All of the corpses and killers are black.

The "graveyard," 3 or 4 acres of smashed brick and twisted tailpipe, lies at the heart of North Philly, the city's black quadrant. People know how to avoid it. The lot is a no man's land between the Valley gang's turf and that of Norris Street. It is a free-fire zone.

Around suppertime one recent evening, mothers set up a loudspeaker on the Valley side. They understood, as did the crowd of thirty or forty, that snipers roam the abandoned houses, called cribs, on the perimeter of the "graveyard." The local strife had claimed eight lives in a little more than a year, and the meeting was meant to protest a recent foray. Earlier in the week, a car from Norris Street had careened through the Valley while a passenger fired a twelve-gauge shotgun. Four small children were wounded at a bus stop.

As in Belfast, raw-lunged mothers decry a life which requires walking children to school, and locking them in the house the rest of the time. Behind in the street, Valley members floated and weaved on "corner-caddies," ten-speed bikes which they hadn't bought with Master Charge. Hard, sleek, and not quite fully grown, they wore T-shirts and jeans, sneakers or work boots. Platform shoes and balloon pants wouldn't work in this world. Hair is pared down or corn-rowed; tiny glass ear studs reflect the light.

A black plain-clothes sergeant from the Gang Control Division stood among the parents with a walkie-talkie. Two others waited in unmarked cars. One of the gang mothers challenged the Valley members to explain the daily fire fights. "You black and they black. We are all poor. So why don't you take your damn gang war out to Kensington?" Kensington is the local version of Boston's Southie. Not so long ago, a house had been fire-bombed there to prevent the first black family from moving in. The gang kids continued to spin mutely in the street.

Suddenly, the crowd twitched. Across the graveyard, four from Norris Street climbed out of a crib and began walking toward us. The unmarked cars hurtled at them, bouncing over rubble. The kids didn't run. Cops emerged guns drawn, frisked them and carted them off. At best, a bad moment was temporarily averted. Six nights later, on Norris turf, Johnny Brown, 17, was assassinated on his stoop on Gratz Street, and Henry Davis, 15, was shot to death as he walked on North Van Pelt, 3 blocks away. The police and the people of both areas suspect that the killer or killers were from the Valley.

Killing engenders a variety of responses from those in and around the gangs. Arnie McNair, 22, sleeps late, because he doesn't have a job and because the Valley doesn't do much until afternoon. McNair attributes his year without work to his gang past. The warring gave him a record; the turf lines made him quit school. Crossing them to get to high school meant regular ambushes. After awhile it became too nerve-racking. His experience is typical. In order to stem the dropout epidemic, a new school probably will rise in the God-awful, but uninhabited and thus neutral, industrial flatlands near the Delaware.

After spending a couple of hours at his girl's place, McNair hit "the Avenue." Columbia Avenue once was black Philadelphia's main strip for food, hock and entertainment. It has always been the spine of McNair's turf. On August 28, 1964, a year to the day after Dr. Martin Luther King announced his dream, one of the decade's first major riots ignited at 22nd and Columbia and eventually engulfed North Philadelphia. The avenue's merchants never returned and the strip remains a boneyard of plywood windows and padlocked grates. But though shoppers have probably gone for good, street life continues. Slack-jawed junkies nod and trade. Gang kids spar, poke about in the rubble and showboat on ten-speeds. Plain-clothes police cruise by in a weird flotilla of bread trucks, Lincolns, VWs and old bombs, fooling no one.

On the day I was with him, McNair hooked up with the bunch from Nineteenth and Montgomery, his old corner, one of six in the Valley. An "old head," retired from the wars, he remains influential because he fought "fair ones" for the gang and did his share of rumbling. He still wears a red rhinestone in his ear. Stitches trail under his eye, a memento of the time he caught a brick with his face. McNair vouched for me, but most of the group of a dozen or so dislike the notion of having a writer around. Why, they ask, should I make money off of their lives and deaths?

Sugar Bear Darden, a 6-foot-5 old head who carries a transistor the size of a radiator and looks as though he could throw a strawberry through a locomotive, more than suggests that I come up with some immediate cash. McNair, a half foot shorter, sides with me and the two begin to "grit" each other.

Before the moment explodes, Butch Pruitt decides that I can stay. Butch is the "runner" or leader (he "runs" the corner). Sugar Bear and the others: Roach, Yogi, Doctor Al, Moonman, Dip—their names on a hundred walls—don't press. Butch, 19, coal black, muscular and sardonic, makes clear that one doesn't become a runner by winning bake-offs. "You got," he says, "to know all the dudes. You got to do some time—I did about two years—and you got to hurt some people." Did he ever kill anyone? "I ain't," he responds, "gonna tell you that."

The group, I realize, is a sort of patrol. Butch steers it through the turf's streets, which are among the city's poorest. The pack expects that someone will try to avenge the deaths on Norris Street. Should they spot an enemy on the turf, Butch says, "He's gonna get croaked. No questions asked. That's survival."

While we talk, police periodically pull up to listen. Valley boys draw local heat the way Dillinger drew the Feds. The gang kids sneer, give the cops the finger and complain to me of brutality. Finally, a measure of privacy is achieved behind a cyclone fence at the Martin Luther King Center, the grim, futurist pool and playground built over the rubble at 22nd and Columbia, where the riot started. The center was intended to benefit and pacify North Philly, but it benefits only those from the Valley, and pacifies no one. The back fence of the playing area is the Norris Street border, which makes the place almost as risky as the graveyard. Because of the exclusivity and danger, the center is eerily underpopulated. Anyone who plays here does so with skittish awareness that someone could be drawing a bead on him.

Butch and the corner boys foresee continued bloodshed. "We got over on Norris Street by two bodies," says Butch. "They gotta strike back till they get even to keep up their reputation. There can't never be peace while somebody's up." He pauses. "To tell you the truth, I ain't through with them myself. They got a bounty on me, and I'd like to drop a bomb on them all."

McNair, once a Black Panther, lobbies for peace. He talks about black killing black, calls it "genocide, just like heroin." "That's solid," Butch comes back, "but there's been too many bodies to stop." Sugar Bear doesn't want me to get the wrong idea. "Oppression brings this on, man. If whites lived under this racism they'd act the same way." He and McNair keep away from each other for the rest of the day. As for the most recent killings, the corner boys speculate that someone from the Valley decided to retaliate for the kid shootings at the bus stop, but they profess not to know who it was.

Until recently, killings were rare. Through the mid-1960s, the city averaged about three gang deaths a year. Before the violence escalated, the Valley was a complex multi-leveled society. Each of its six corners had a variety of gang officials in addition to runners. A warlord led the gang in rumbles. There were judges as well as diplomats. The latter, called "check holders," made treaties and organized "fair ones"—weaponless fights between a Valley member and another gang's "jitterbug" to settle inter-turf disputes. Violence, an element of policy, was planned at the top.

Today, there are only runners, and the gang has no treaties, rumbles, or fair ones. Jitterbugs decide on their own when and how to vent their wrath. The average age of gang killers and corpses in this city is sixteen and a half. The corner boys feel that there are fewer officials because police spot leaders for harassment and arrest. Frank Rizzo's articulated policy, both as Police Commissioner and as Mayor, has been to put the gang leaders behind bars. Indeed, in recent years enough have been jailed to organize a turf-by-turf microcosm of the city in all local detention facilities. Curiously, in prison, where it is at least as easy to kill as on the street, fair ones and beatings are the predominant ways of handling conflict.

Leaderlessness explains why jitterbugs make decisions regarding violence, but it doesn't explain their preference for deadly quick "hits." In fact, gang members seem confused by the trend to homicide. The corner boys mainly respond obtusely when I ask about their roles in the war. One, Yogi Bethea, a slight, smooth-faced 15-year-old, shyly admits to being a night shooter, a fact which troubles him. Yogi knows he'll die: "I'll be standin' on my corner. The car'll pull up to me and the window'll roll down. That's the last thing I'll see."

Yogi had mainly kept his nose clean until 1973, when his cousin was killed. "In the old days," he says, "we would've rocked steady, but nobody rumbles now." It wasn't easy to get a gun. He had to break into two houses before he found the .38 which he shares with five others and hides in a moldering crib. Last summer his rage doubled when his corner boy was gored with a file.

Arnie McNair senses that Yogi is about to become a statistic. He arranges to take him for a ride in his stepfather's car to Germantown, Fairmount Park, anywhere away from the tension. A Valley jitterbug can't walk safely across turf lines in any direction. "Around here," rues Yogi who needs some time away to collect himself, "you can't hide. Somebody's always watchin' you."

"Dudes' minds," says McNair later, "are getting blowed left and right."

To its credit, Philadelphia hasn't ignored the violence. Anti–gang war conferences, reports, bumper stickers and TV spots (young super-flies confined to wheelchairs) abound. The city pays 400 employees—cops, social workers and others—to grapple specifically with the problem at an annual figure in excess of $5 million. Since summer, I've talked to many of these people as well as to journalists and politicians. All seem to be at a loss to explain why the gangs turned to killing.

My impression is that the city's strategy has had a great deal to do with the change. Using the wrong tool can disastrously worsen a mess. One doesn't use a jackhammer to unclog a drain; the United States shouldn't have applied its military to Vietnam. Philadelphia's approach to gang violence has been heavy surveillance. Wrong tool.

The Gang Control Division, which grew from fifteen to ninety officers in the past decade, spearheads the effort, which also increasingly involves members of police in the districts (who receive much information directly from Gang Control), City Hall's patrol force and the social workers. No one would deny that the surveillance has been successful in determining the number of violent gangs, their memberships and leaders, or that it has led to an ever growing number of arrests.

But though statistical information on the gangs is generally sketchy, some figures are clear, disturbing and borne out by the reality of the street. In 1963, when Gang Control was able to monitor twenty-seven violent gangs, there were four homicides. Reported violence mainly took the form of rumbles, of which there were forty-six. There were only thirteen shootings.

In ensuing years the number of fighting gangs under observation steadily increased. By the 1970s, all 105 were being watched. In the same years the number of shootings rose dramatically and the number of rumbles plummeted. In 1973, there were forty-three gang deaths, 159 shootings, and only seven rumbles.

A gang shooting is fast, low-visibility violence. It requires one gunman and a moment under cover of night. By comparison, a rumble is slow and highly visible. Scores of fighters must be drafted from around the turf and funneled to a designated spot where the commotion they create isn't exactly subtle. Effective surveillance makes rumbling nearly impossible. Doubtless, it also accounts for the extinction of fair ones. The result has been a tragic shift to "hits." Where causes of gang violence such as revenge, reputation and territory remain, heavy surveillance doesn't eliminate the violence; it merely speeds it up.

To the black community, in particular, the yearly Attica-scale destruction of young males remains horrifyingly incomprehensible. But, of course, the mothers, lovers and families of Richard Taylor, Henry Davis, Johnny Brown, and all the other wasted 16- and 17-year-olds must be given some sort of explanation, something to go on. The first and last time I saw Johnny Brown, he was wearing a tuxedo and a smile. His Afro had been shaped into a dark halo. The bullet hole in his head was undetectable.

The train of viewers took an hour to file past the brass box. Johnny's mother collapsed; the mother of his two children moaned hysterically. His corner boys took a hard look, then left. In front of the hall, they stood arms folded, beret-clad, ready for marauders from the Valley. Because coffins have been tipped and corpses mutilated, some funeral directors refuse to put up gang bodies. Three prowl cars were on the scene.

The talk of the Norris Street boys is ironic, tragic, familiar. They say they want to stop the war, but that the Valley keeps coming since it's still three bodies down from last year. It's the same "getting even" line I've heard on Columbia Avenue, but the time standard has been changed. Unanimously, they lament the age of gun war, wish they still could fight fair ones, and wonder why the form has perished.

As in the Valley, the hierarchy has broken down. Even runners have disappeared from Norris Street. Two years ago a cop was killed on the turf by gang kids, and it is likely there is a connection. I imagine it would be impossible to be a runner on Norris Street today, for all the police attention one would receive.

Inside the hall, as family and neighbors choke and wail, a small black-robed woman, the Reverend Hattie Hays, belts out the undying Baptism of the Deep South. "Don't cry mother, don't cry father," she commands. "This is not a sad day but a happy day. You loved little Johnny, but Jesus loves him more." People shout "amen." Some fall to their knees.

"There are trials and tribulations for our boys out here," she continues. "And more will fall. More will fall for God is callin'." The explanation eases the heart if not the mind. The wailing rises until it shakes the hall.

Two weeks after the funeral, a body which had been dragged is found on Sixteenth Street, the border between the Valley and Oxford Street. Apparently, the boy, a 17-year-old from Oxford turf, had gone into the Valley looking to make a hit and had been shot instead. He could have intended to avenge Johnny Brown, or maybe he had another score to settle. It's unfortunate that he couldn't have found himself a rumble or a fair one. Chances are, he would have survived it.

~ 1989 ~

Crime, Drugs & the Media: The Black Pathology Biz

Ishmael Reed

Novelist Ishmael Reed's many books include *Mumbo Jumbo* and *The Terrible Twos*. He was chair of PEN's Oakland media committee when he wrote this article.

NOVEMBER 20, 1989 ~ Black pathology is big business. Two-thirds of teenage mothers are white, two-thirds of welfare recipients are white and white youth commit most of the crime in this country. According to a recent survey, reported by the Oakland *Tribune*, the typical crack addict is a middle-class white male in his 40s. Michele Norris of *The Washington Post* has cited a study that discovered "no significant difference in the rate of drug use during pregnancy among women in the public clinics that serve a largely indigent population and those visiting private doctors who cater to upper-income patients." Yet in the popular imagination blacks are blamed for all these activities, in the manner that the Jews took the rap for the Black Plague, even in countries with little or no Jewish population.

Now that network news shows have become "profit centers," news producers have found a lucrative market in exhibiting black pathology, while coverage of pathologies such as drug addiction, child abuse, spousal battering and crime among whites and their "model minorities" is negligible. According to the news shows, you'd think that two black gangs, the Crips and the Bloods, are both the cause and the result of the nation's drug problem, even though this country was high long before these children were born.

When it comes to singling out blacks as the cause of America's social problems, NBC and CNN are the worst offenders. (The owner of CNN, Ted Turner, once proposed that unemployed black males be hired to carry nuclear warheads on their backs; when pressed he said that he was only kidding.)

Let's look at just one month: October of last year. General Electric's *NBC Nightly News* ran stories on child abuse, drug trafficking and cocaine pregnancy. Blacks were the actors in all these news shows, yet the

August 30, 1988, front page of *The New York Times* reported that there is as much cocaine pregnancy in the suburbs as in the inner city. That same October, it was revealed on CNN's business program, *Moneyline*, that U.S. bankers have laundered $100 billion in drug money, $90 billion of which ends up overseas, contributing to the trillion dollars in debt owed by the United States, mugging millions of Americans of jobs and endangering the economic stability of the country.

Also in October, CNN did a series called "Crime in America." According to this series, whites don't commit crimes. They're either victims or on the side of the law—the line promoted by *The New York Times*, a black pathology supermarket that regularly blames crack use, crime, welfare and illegitimacy on black people and whose journalists and columnists still use the term "black underclass" even though studies, including *Blacks and American Society*, by the National Research Council, and *The Persistence of Urban Poverty and its Demographic and Behavioral Correlates*, by Terry K. Adams and Greg J. Duncan, have been unable to locate this underclass. Its neoconservative house organ, *The New York Times Magazine*, printed in its February 26 issue a puff piece about the ex-editors of the anti-Semitic, anti-black *Dartmouth Review*.

Earlier last year, on August 20, CNN aired a special about drug-crazed Los Angeles street gangs. It proposed that gang activities were inspired by rap music. If rap music is forcing people to sell drugs, then how does one explain the participation in this industry of a Gregorian chant–loving ex-Vatican diplomat, the Rev. Lorenzo Zorza?

How convenient it is to blame everything on a scapegoat, in this case black youth, who, according to public superstitions, are responsible for all the crime in this country. Yet Gerry Spence, citing a Bureau of National Affairs estimate, writes in his book *With Justice for None: Destroying an American Myth*, that "the cost of corporate crime in America is over ten times greater than the combined larcenies, robberies, burglaries and auto-thefts committed by individuals. One in five of America's large corporations has been convicted of at least one major crime or has paid civil penalties for serious misbehavior. One way the Crips and the Bloods can improve their image is to do what the big crooks do, buy advertising on TV news shows so that their crimes will rarely be reported." The only difference between white pathology and black pathology is that white pathology is underreported.

By putting out the lie that U.S. crime is black, the networks contributed millions of dollars in free advertising to Lee Atwater's most recent racist political campaign.

Presenting the fact that pathologies are widespread in American society and that American society itself might be pathological would be like showing films about lung cancer to the millions addicted to cigarette smoking. To portray America as a pathological society would interrupt the country's cozy fetal sleep, which requires that the shrill half-wits it elects to office run the sort of campaign that former Confederate officers ran in the 1880s: They threatened whites with a black rapist in every bedroom, an image that's been commercialized by some millionaire feminists in novels and movies for the last decade, proving that the black pathology industry is an equal-opportunity gold mine.

~ 1 9 9 2 ~

In L.A., Burning All Illusions

Mike Davis

Mike Davis is the author, most recently, of *City of Quartz: Excavating the Future in Los Angeles* (Vintage), and is a *Nation* contributing editor.

Los Angeles

JUNE 1, 1992 ~ The armored personnel carrier squats on the corner like an *un gran sapo feo*—"a big ugly toad"—according to 9-year-old Emerio. His parents talk anxiously, almost in a whisper, about the *desaparecidos*: Raul from Tepic, big Mario, the younger Flores girl and the cousin from Ahuachapan. Like all Salvadorans, they know about those who "disappear"; they remember the headless corpses and the man whose tongue had been pulled through the hole in his throat like a necktie. That is why they came here—to ZIP code 90057, Los Angeles, California.

Now they are counting their friends and neighbors, Salvadoran and Mexican, who are suddenly gone. Some are still in the County Jail on Bauchet Street, little more than brown grains of sand lost among the 17,000 other alleged *saqueadores* (looters) and *incendarios* (arsonists) detained after the most violent American civil disturbance since the Irish poor burned Manhattan in 1863. Those without papers are probably already back in Tijuana, broke and disconsolate, cut off from their families and new lives. Violating city policy, the police fed hundreds of hapless undocumented *saqueadores* to the I.N.S. for deportation before the A.C.L.U. or immigrant rights groups even realized they had been arrested.

For many days the television talked only of the "South Central riot," "black rage" and the "Crips and Bloods." But Emerio's parents know that thousands of their neighbors from the MacArthur Park district—home to nearly one-tenth of all the Salvadorans in the world—also looted, burned, stayed out past curfew and went to jail. (An analysis of the first 5,000 arrests from all over the city revealed that 52 percent were poor Latinos, 10 percent whites and only 38 percent blacks.) They also know that the nation's first multiracial riot was as much about empty bellies and broken hearts as it was about police batons and Rodney King.

The week before the riot was unseasonably hot. At night the people lingered outside on the stoops and sidewalks of their tenements (MacArthur

Park is L.A.'s Spanish Harlem), talking about their new burden of trouble. In a neighborhood far more crowded than mid-Manhattan and more dangerous than downtown Detroit, with more crack addicts and gangbangers than registered voters, *la gente* know how to laugh away every disaster except the final one. Yet there was a new melancholy in the air.

Too many people have been losing their jobs: their *pinche* $5.25-an-hour jobs as seamstresses, laborers, busboys and factory workers. In two years of recession, unemployment has tripled in L.A.'s immigrant neighborhoods. At Christmas more than 20,000 predominantly Latina women and children from throughout the central city waited all night in the cold to collect a free turkey and a blanket from charities. Other visible barometers of distress are the rapidly growing colonies of homeless *compañeros* on the desolate flanks of Crown Hill and in the concrete bed of the L.A. River, where people are forced to use sewage water for bathing and cooking.

As mothers and fathers lose their jobs, or as unemployed relatives move under the shelter of the extended family, there is increasing pressure on teenagers to supplement the family income. Belmont High School is the pride of "Little Central America," but with nearly 4,500 students it is severely overcrowded, and an additional 2,000 students must be bused to distant schools in the San Fernando Valley and elsewhere. Fully 7,000 school-age teenagers in the Belmont area, moreover, have dropped out of school. Some have entered the *vida loca* of gang culture (there are 100 different gangs in the school district that includes Belmont High), but most are struggling to find minimum-wage footholds in a declining economy.

The neighbors in MacArthur Park whom I interviewed, such as Emerio's parents, all speak of this gathering sense of unease, a perception of a future already looted. The riot arrived like a magic dispensation. People were initially shocked by the violence, then mesmerized by the televised image of biracial crowds in South Central L.A. helping themselves to mountains of desirable goods without interference from the police. The next day, Thursday, April 30, the authorities blundered twice: first by suspending school and releasing the kids into the streets; second by announcing that the National Guard was on the way to help enforce a dusk-to-dawn curfew.

Thousands immediately interpreted this as a last call to participate in the general redistribution of wealth in progress. Looting spread with explosive force throughout Hollywood and MacArthur Park, as well as parts of Echo Park, Van Nuys and Huntington Park. Although arsonists spread terrifying destruction, the looting crowds were governed by a visible moral economy. As one middle-aged lady explained to me, "Stealing is a sin, but this is like a television game show where everyone in the audience gets to win." Unlike the looters in Hollywood (some on skateboards) who stole Madonna's bustier and all the crotchless panties from Frederick's, the masses of MacArthur Park concentrated on the prosaic necessities of life like cockroach spray and Pampers.

Now, one week later, MacArthur Park is in a state of siege. A special "We Tip" hotline invites people to inform on neighbors or acquaintances suspected of looting. Elite L.A.P.D. Metro Squad units, supported by the National Guard, sweep through the tenements in search of stolen goods, while Border Patrolmen from as far away as Texas prowl the streets. Frantic parents search for missing kids, like mentally retarded 14-year-old Zuly Estrada, who is believed to have been deported to Mexico.

Meanwhile, thousands of *saqueadores*, many of them pathetic scavengers captured in the charred ruins the day after the looting, languish in County Jail, unable to meet absurdly high bails. One man, caught with a packet of sunflower seeds and two cartons of milk, is being held on $15,000; hundreds of others face felony indictments and possible two-year prison terms. Prosecutors demand thirty-day jail sentences for curfew violators, despite the fact that many of those are either homeless street people or Spanish-speakers who were unaware of the curfew. These are the "weeds" that George Bush says we must pull from the soil of our cities before it can be sown with the regenerating "seeds" of enterprise zones and tax breaks for private capital.

"Little Gangster" Tak can't get over his amazement that he is actually standing in the same room of Brother Aziz's mosque with a bunch of Inglewood Crips. The handsome, 22-year-old Tak, a "straight up" Inglewood Blood who looks more like a black angel by Michelangelo than one of the Boyz N the Hood, still has two Crip bullets in his body, and "they still carry a few of mine." Some of the Crips and Bloods, whose blue or red gang colors have been virtual tribal flags, remember one another from school playground days, but mainly they have met over the barrels of automatics in a war that has divided Inglewood—the pleasant, black-majority city southwest of L.A. where the Lakers play—by a river of teenage blood. Now, as Tak explains, "Everybody knows what time it is. If we don't end the killing now and unite as black men, we never will."

Although Imam Aziz and the Nation of Islam have provided the formal auspices for peacemaking, the real hands that have "tied the red and blue rags together into a 'black thang'" are in Simi Valley. Within a few hours of the first attack on white motorists, which started in 8-Trey (83rd Street) Gangster Crip territory near Florence and Normandie, the insatiable war between the Crips and Bloods, fueled by a thousand neighborhood vendettas and dead homeboys, was "put on hold" throughout Los Angeles and the adjacent black suburbs of Compton and Inglewood.

Unlike the 1965 rebellion, which broke out south of Watts and remained primarily focused on the poorer east side of the ghetto, the 1992 riot reached its maximum temperature along Crenshaw Boulevard—the very heart of black Los Angeles's more affluent west side. Despite the illusion of full-immersion "actuality" provided by the minicam and the helicopter, television's coverage of the riot's angry edge was even more twisted than the melted steel of Crenshaw's devastated shopping centers. Most reporters—"image looters" as they are now being called in South Central—merely lip-synched suburban clichés as they tramped through the ruins of lives they had no desire to understand. A violent kaleidoscope of bewildering complicity was flattened into a single, categorical scenario: legitimate black anger over the King decision hijacked by hard-core street criminals and transformed into a maddened assault on their own community.

Local television thus unwittingly mimed the McCone Commission's summary judgment that the August 1965 Watts riot was primarily the act of a hoodlum fringe. In that case, a subsequent U.C.L.A. study revealed that the "riot of the riffraff" was in fact a popular uprising involving at least 50,000 working-class adults and their teenage children. When the arrest records of this latest uprising are finally analyzed, they will probably also vindicate the judgment of many residents that all segments of black youth, gang and non-gang, "buppie" as well as underclass, took part in the disorder.

Although in Los Angeles, as elsewhere, the new black middle class has socially and spatially pulled farther apart from the deindustrialized black working class, the L.A.P.D.'s Operation Hammer and other antigang dragnets that arrested kids at random (entering their names and addresses into an electronic gang roster that is now proving useful in house-to-house searches for riot "ringleaders") have tended to criminalize black youth without class distinction. Between 1987 and 1990, the combined sweeps of the L.A.P.D. and the County Sheriff's Office ensnared 50,000 "suspects." Even the children of doctors and lawyers from View Park and Windsor Hills have had to "kiss the pavement" and occasionally endure some of the humiliations that the homeboys in the flats face every day—experiences that reinforce the reputation of the gangs (and their poets laureate, the gangster rappers like Ice Cube and N.W.A.) as the heroes of an outlaw generation.

Yet if the riot had a broad social base, it was the partcipation of the gangs—or, rather, their cooperation—that gave it constant momentum and direction. If the 1965 rebellion was a hurricane, leveling one hundred blocks of Central Avenue from Vernon to lmperial Highway, the 1992 riot was a tornado, no less destructive but snaking a zigzag course through the commercial areas of the ghetto and beyond. Most of the media saw no pattern in its path, just blind, nihilistic destruction. In fact, the arson was ruthlessly systematic. By Friday morning 90 percent of the myriad Korean-owned liquor stores, markets and swapmeets in South Central L.A. had been wiped out. Deserted by the L.A.P.D., which made no attempt to defend small businesses, the Koreans suffered damage or destruction to almost 2,000 stores from Compton to the heart of Koreatown itself. One of the first to be attacked (although, ironically, it survived) was the grocery store where 15-year-old Latasha Harlins was shot in the back of the head last year by Korean grocer Soon Ja Du in a dispute over a $1.79 bottle of orange juice. The girl died with the money for her purchase in her hand.

Latasha Harlins. A name that was scarcely mentioned on television was the key to the catastrophic collapse of relations between L.A.'s black and Korean communities. Ever since white judge Joyce Karlin let Du off with a $500 fine and some community service—a sentence which declared that the taking of a black child's life was scarcely more serious than drunk driving—some interethnic explosion has been virtually inevitable. The several near-riots at the Compton courthouse this winter were early warning signals of the black community's unassuaged grief over Harlins's murder. On the streets of South Central Wednesday and Thursday, I was repeatedly told, "This is for our baby sister. This is for Latasha."

The balance of grievances in the community is complex. Rodney King is the symbol that links unleashed police racism in Los Angeles to the crisis of black life everywhere, from Las Vegas to Toronto. Indeed, it is becoming clear that the King case may be almost as much of a watershed in American history as Dred Scott, a test of the very meaning of the citizenship for which African-Americans have struggled for 400 years.

But on the grass-roots level, especially among gang youth, Rodney King may not have quite the same profound resonance. As one of the Inglewood Bloods told me: "Rodney King? Shit, my homies be beat like dogs by the police every day. This riot is about all the homeboys murdered by the police, about the little sister killed by the Koreans, about twenty-seven years of oppression. Rodney King just the trigger."

At the same time, those who predicted that the next L.A. riot would be a literal Armageddon have been proved wrong. Despite a thousand Day-Glo exhortations on the walls of South Central to "Kill the Police," the gangs have refrained from the deadly guerrilla warfare that they are so formidably equipped to conduct. As in 1965, there has not been a single L.A.P.D. fatality, and indeed few serious police injuries of any kind.

In this round, at least, the brunt of gang power was directed toward the looting and destruction of the Korean stores. If Latasha Harlins is the impassioned pretext, there may be other agendas as well. I saw graffiti in South Central that advocated "Day one: burn them out. Day two: we rebuild." The only national leader whom most Crips and Bloods seem to take seriously is Louis Farrakhan, and his goal of black economic self-determination is broadly embraced. (Farrakhan, it should be emphasized, has never advocated violence as a means to this end.) At the Inglewood gang summit, which took place on May 5, there were repeated references to a renaissance of black capitalism out of the ashes of Korean businesses. "After all," an ex-Crip told me later, "we didn't burn our community, just *their* stores."

In the meantime, the police and military occupiers of Los Angeles give no credence to any peaceful, let alone entrepreneurial, transformation of L.A.'s black gang cultures. The ecumenical movement of the Crips and Bloods is their worst imagining: gang violence no longer random but politicized into a black *intifada*. The L.A.P.D. remembers only too well that a generation ago the Watts rebellion produced a gang peace out of which grew the Los Angeles branch of the Black Panther Party. As if to prove their suspicions, the police have circulated a copy of an anonymous and possibly spurious leaflet calling for gang unity and "an eye for an eye. . . . If L.A.P.D. hurt a black we'll kill two."

For its part, the Bush Administration has federalized the repression in L.A. with an eye to the spectacle of the President marching in triumph, like a Roman emperor, with captured Crips and Bloods in chains. Thus, the Justice Department has dispatched to L.A. the same elite task force of federal marshals who captured Manuel Noriega in Panama as reinforcements for L.A.P.D. and F.B.I. efforts to track down the supposed gang instigators of the riot. But as a veteran of the 1965 riot said while watching SWAT teams arrest some of the hundreds of rival gang members trying to meet peacefully at Watts's Jordan Downs Housing Project: "That ole fool Bush think we as dumb as Saddam. Land Marines in Compton and get hisself re-elected. But this ain't Iraq. This is Vietnam, Jack."

A core grievance fueling the Watts rebellion and the subsequent urban insurrections of 1967-68 was rising black unemployment in the midst of a boom economy. What contemporary journalists fearfully described as the beginning of the "Second Civil War" was as much a protest against black America's exclusion from the military-Keynesian expansion of the 1960s as it was an uprising against police racism and de facto segregation in schools and housing. The 1992 riot and its possible progenies must likewise be understood as insurrections against an intolerable political-economic order. As even the *Los Angeles Times*, main cheerleader for "World City L.A.," now editorially acknowledges, the "globalization of Los Angeles" has produced "devastating poverty for those weak in skills and resources."

Although the $1 billion worth of liquor stores and mini-malls destroyed in L.A. may seem like chump change next to the $2.6 trillion recently annihilated on the Tokyo Stock Exchange, the burning of Oz probably fits into the same Hegelian niche with the bursting of the Bubble Economy: not the "end of history" at the seacoast of Malibu but the beginning of an ominous dialectic on the rim of the Pacific. It was a hallucination in the first place to imagine that the wheel of the world economy could be turned indefinitely by a Himalaya of U.S. trade deficits and a fictitious yen.

This structural crisis of the Japan-California "co-prosperity sphere," however, threatens to translate class contradictions into interethnic conflict on both the national and local level. Culturally distinct "middleman" groups—ethnic entrepreneurs and the like—risk being seen as the personal representatives of the invisible hand that has looted local communities of economic autonomy. In the ease of Los Angeles, it was tragically the neighborhood Korean liquor store, not the skyscraper corporate fortress downtown, that became the symbol of a despised new world order.

On their side, the half-million Korean-Americans in L.A. have been psychologically lacerated by the failure of the state to protect them against black rage. Indeed, several young Koreans told me that they were especially bitter that the South Central shopping malls controlled by Alexander Haagen, a wealthy contributor to local polities, were quickly defended by police and National Guard, while their stores were leisurely ransacked and burned to the ground. "Maybe this is what we get," a U.C.L.A. student said, "for uncritically buying into the white middle class's attitude toward blacks and its faith in the police."

The prospects for a multicultural reconciliation in Los Angeles depend much less on white knight Peter Ueberroth's committee of corporate rebuilders than upon a general economic recovery in Southern California. As the Los Angeles *Business Journal* complained (after noting that L.A. had lost 100,000 manufacturing jobs over the past three years), "The riots are like poison administered to a sick patient."

Forecasts still under wraps at the Southern California Association of Governments paint a dark future for the Land of Sunshine, as job growth, slowed by the decline of aerospace as well as manufacturing shifts to Mexico, lags far behind population increase. Unemployment rates—not counting the estimated 40,000 jobs lost from the riot, and the uprising's impact on the business climate—are predicted to remain at 8 to 10 percent (and 40 to 50 percent for minority youth) for the next generation, while the housing crisis, already the most acute in the nation, will spill over into new waves of homelessness. Thus, the "widening divide" of income inequality in Los Angeles County, described in a landmark 1988 study by U.C.L.A. professor Paul Ong, will become an unbridgeable chasm. Southern California's endless summer is finally over.

Affluent Angelenos instinctively sensed this as they patrolled their Hancock Park estates with shotguns or bolted in their BMWs for white sanctuaries in Orange and Ventura counties. From Palm Springs poolsides they anxiously awaited news of the burning of Beverly Hills by the Crips and Bloods, and fretted over the extra set of house keys they had foolishly entrusted to the Latina maid. Was she now an incendiarist? Although their fears were hysterically magnified, tentacles of disorder did penetrate such sanctums of white life as the Beverly Center and Westwood Village, as well as the Melrose and Fairfax neighborhoods. Most alarmingly, the L.A.P.D.'s "thin blue line," which had protected them in 1965, was now little more than a defunct metaphor, the last of Chief Gates's bad jokes.

~ 1995 ~

America and the Simpson Trial

Patricia J. Williams

Patricia J. Williams, a professor at Columbia Law School and a *Nation* contributing editor is the author of *The Alchemy of Race and Rights* (Harvard).

MARCH 13, 1995 ~ There was a story some years ago about a penitentiary in Texas where state prison officials asked inmates to volunteer to help train their tracking dogs. The inmates would be dressed up in padded clothing, given a head start, and then the hungry hounds would be loosed, with the prison officials riding on horseback after them. It became quite a sport, the chasing of what they called the "dog boys," and it eventually embarrassed (though scarcely enough) quite a number of politicians (who had joined in the frolic) when the degree to which it had become a jolly pastime, like fox-hunting, came to public light.

The degree to which official exercises of power become major-league sports events gives me a lot of pause these days, as I cautiously turn on the television from time to time, searching for the weather report while trying to avoid the swamp of O.J. Simpson mania. Sooner or later, I fear, it will sweep me away too, in the excruciatingly slow, molasses-motioned displacement of afternoon soap opera by the industrial-strength suds of *Court TV* opera.

Although I had promised myself that I would be the one lawyer in the United States to refrain from writing about the Simpson case, I'm increasingly troubled by the way it severely pushes the limits of whatever justice was supposed to be afforded by the notion of a public trial. The unprecedented eclipse of trial by theater—rivaled only perhaps by the coverage of Dr. Sam Sheppard in the 1950s—has whetted a public appetite for lurid speculation as well as spectacle. It is an appetite, I fear, that will be satisfied by neither a guilty *nor* a not-guilty verdict, for surely so much melodrama is building to a better denouement than *that*. The public wants great pulp fiction: say, for Marcia Clark to have Johnnie Cochran's baby while O.J. and Detective Fuhrman commit suicide in a double homosexual interracial love pact, and just for good measure Judge Ito is discovered to be heading up an international cocaine cartel whose operations he directs from his chambers during the commercial breaks.

Of course, this is why juries get sequestered—it's a way of limiting not the public viewing of the trial but the mob's metaphoric climbing-into-the-witness-box and influencing the outcome by noisy, string-'em-up gladiatorial rhetoric and rumor-run-amok.

Still troubling to the unsequestered of us, however, might be the extent to which the public airing of the Simpson trial is being used to divert political attention from some very great divisions rending this nation. "Maybe the Simpson trial will undo the misperceptions created by the Rodney King thing," said one commentator on a morning news show—barely two days after publication of the Mollen Commission report, which detailed police excesses in Harlem and the Bronx, including racketeering, narcotics dealing and even attempted murder. This seemingly pervasive sentiment astonishes me for a number of reasons: It reduces black anxiety about the justice system to superficial and singular television encounters—the Rodney King "thing" may have "created" a bad impression, but look, "the system" is apologizing, by making up for it with O.J. Simpson. It trivializes or ignores the day-to-day experiences of blacks who are treated as "suspect profiles" at best and suffer a range of abuses in contacts with the justice system that go from negligence to outright brutality. And it dangerously misreads the discontent of a significant population that is not merely disaffected but enraged, whose fury is barely reflected in the staggering rates of black criminalization and imprisonment.

The O.J. Simpson trial bears very little resemblance to the circumstances—in courtrooms or elsewhere—that occasion so much black distrust of the justice system. But the self-congratulation proceeds apace: *Now* maybe *they* will see that justice is color-blind, say so many of the high-priced pundits who crowd the airwaves. Yeah yeah, except all sides agree that this trial is hardly typical. How many black or white people can afford a team of defense lawyers like O.J.'s? How many black or white people could command the audience that he does? How many black men could lead the Los Angeles Police Department on a slow chase around the city and survive to spawn a publishing industry of True! Inside! stories, all sure to be best sellers?

The Simpson coverage takes a singular trial—possibly one of the most bizarre of the century—and mythologizes it into the mundane. The simultaneous failure to cover the Mollen Commission report with anything like the same spotlight allows such mythologizing to trump empiricism in dangerous ways. And when the empirical becomes so thoroughly disconnected from political belief structures, it's a formula for social tension.

"Do you think blacks will riot if O.J. Simpson is found guilty?" a reporter asked me during the preliminary hearing. The question made me laugh. "Are you serious?" I asked before I realized that he was. Of course, the last laugh may turn out to be on me, but it still seems preposterous that anyone could think that angry black crowds would storm the streets—of what, Brentwood?—just because *a black man* was found guilty. The question struck me as revealing a total lack of understanding of the riotous passion that caused the infuriated, blind eruptions in Los Angeles—as though the reporter expected that anytime any black man is convicted, no matter what he does, black communities will scream foul. What a total lack of understanding of the seething social desperation that the Simi Valley verdict blew open.

Even acknowledging that there are plenty of blacks who don't believe that any black man can get a fair trial in the United States, those beliefs alone hardly cause riots. How random and shallow the discontent must seem if O.J. Simpson is made the measure of black oppression, just another example of *playing the race card.*

If O.J. Simpson is believed by many whites to be enjoying the typical trial of a black man (you know, mired in the indulgences of due process, time-consuming and more expensive than the national budget), then Colin Ferguson, the man who opened fire on a crowded car on the Long Island Rail Road, has been figured as the typical black man (you know, always complaining, always blaming, paranoid). I don't know how to say this gracefully, but there's paranoia and there's paranoia, and Colin Ferguson is *insane.* He thinks there are ninety-three counts against him because the year of the shooting was 1993. He was sleeping at the time. Mario Cuomo is part of a plot to set him up. The witnesses are all lying and the dead aren't really dead. Yet a judge found him competent to stand trial and all the headlines self-righteously proclaimed his raising of that old defense, The white man did it. *That's what they all say! Well, he's crazy if he thinks we'll believe that one!* Isn't there something completely upside down about ruling an insane man sane so that society can waggle their heads and call him insane? The oft-paired but fundamentally contradictory logic is: He's just acting this way to convince the court that he's crazy. That is, he's plotted and planned his insanity. Doing insane things just proves the demonic rationality of his warped but "normal" paranoid black mind. What is the function, one must begin to wonder as he babbles and soars in a world of his own, of "normal"-izing Ferguson as the quintessential black mind?

Meanwhile, in the not-too-distant background, Susan Smith, who confessed to killing her children after precipitating a nationwide manhunt when she told authorities a black man did it, is figured as someone who is guilty as sin but simultaneously filled with pluck and remorse, ready to shoulder her full "responsibility" by stepping right on up to the electric chair like a pitcher to the mound.

What are these stories we are telling ourselves? We can't sequester the public imagination, but shouldn't we be just a little more careful in how we rush to mythologize our fears, our demons, our mental inventions? Shouldn't we be a little more careful about digging ourselves deeper into the entrenchment of our division?

Would it help to make a reality checklist? A scorecard of sorts, just to keep the myths trimmed, like fingernails, every so often, so they don't get dangerous or poke someone's eyes out or just plain paralyze us?

§ The Simpson trial is hardly the normal trial of a black man, even though it symbolizes the domestic abuse of many "normal" citizens, black and white.

§ Colin Ferguson is not your average black man, even though he expresses fears of the white world that are familiar to many blacks.

§ Blacks who talk a lot about social inequities are not per se insane, even though I appreciate that there are many white people who find them very annoying.

§ Colin Ferguson is not your average urban American terrorist. In fact, until Ferguson, the suspect profile of those who went into public places and shot randomly was the lonely, reclusive or recently divorced, troubled, middle-aged white man.

§ If Susan Smith does die in the electric chair and O.J. Simpson doesn't, perhaps we as a nation could refrain just a moment before intoning that white women die for their crimes while black men who commit double homicides don't. Perhaps we could just make room for a host of competing considerations such as: A woman who kills her children is always more abhorred than a man who kills his wife in the so-called "heat of passion" and/or kills a man he thinks is his wife's lover. The death penalty is administered variously by state governments, differently in South Carolina and California. Seeking the death penalty is a matter of prosecutorial discretion. O.J. is a star, dadgummit, and nobody likes to see American heroes executed. If O.J. were "Willie" Horton, he'd fry. And if Susan Smith had murdered almost anyone but her own children, she probably would not.

§ Blacks and Latinos form a solid majority of our national prison population. They are convicted more frequently and sentenced for longer terms than their white counterparts. Blacks end up on death row in numbers vastly disproportionate to whites who commit the same crimes.

Now that all the boxes are checked off, are these factors really a source of comfort to those who think that black men are out there "getting away" with things while white women, even murderesses, are out there doing their bit to uphold the social order? Or shouldn't this complicated play between exceptionalizing trends and normalizing extremes give us a *frisson* of a decidedly more sinister sort? How does a democratic order rationalize the craving for catharsis that countenances this savage running of the bulls, this chasing of the dog boy, this stoning of the one marked village idiot? These are not times for easy prescriptions, but when the executives of *Entertainment Tonight* are *this* exuberant, one has to wonder if Justice hasn't been just a wee bit seduced by the thrill of the hunt.

Chapter Two

~

BARS & BARRIERS: THE POLITICS OF THE COLOR LINE

The Thirteenth Juror

April 26, 1933 by Mary Rose

~ 1 9 1 0 ~

The Negro and the Unions

Oswald Garrison Villard

Oswald Garrison Villard, who in 1909 helped found the
N.A.A.C.P., served as editor of *The Nation* from 1918 to
1932.

December 1, 1910 ~ Mr. Gompers, in a telegram to the National
Association for the Advancement of Colored People, made haste to deny
that in his recent speech before the Federation of Labor Convention he had
said "anything derogatory to the negro race or proposed to read the negro
out of the labor movement." As reported, he had conveyed the impression
that he wanted all negroes eliminated from unions because we could not
expect "a people with all their traditions tending to tear down, to understand the fundamental philosophy of human rights; this is not a theory but a
condition with which we have to deal." Not unnaturally, from Booker
Washington down there have been protests. If the labor-union movement
has any justification, it is because it intends or was originally intended to aid
those classes least able to help themselves, the classes beset by ignorance
and prejudice and exploited by greed and cunning. It is precisely for these
reasons and the inability of the working women to vote that the movement
to organize women workers in unions has been making headway in New
York City.

If to become a philosopher first is essential to the acquirement of a
union card, it is obvious that many cards would have to be revoked. Labor
unions that draw the color-line or refuse admission to Italians or other
nationalities give the lie to the union assertion that theirs is a movement for
true economic equality and genuine democracy. But if Mr. Gompers denies
that he attacked the negro race and wished to exclude them from the
unions, there is nothing in his utterances at St. Louis or elsewhere which

we have seen that indicates an earnest desire to enroll many negroes among his supporters or to give them a real welcome. He dwells upon the difficulties of handling the colored workers; he does not seem to declare that these are precisely the difficulties the union movement likes to grapple with and meet. As a matter of fact, his attitude reflects, in the main, that of the unions throughout the country. Few welcome the negro with open arms, though there are some that do so, notably in the mining districts of Alabama. Some, like the engineers' union on the Central of Georgia Railway, would confine him to the lowest grade of engine-labor, while others, particularly in the North, are sullenly indifferent, or admit only a few men of color, if any.

So far as the American Federation of Labor is concerned, it originally took the position that it would admit no union which discriminated in its charter against the colored man. But that high ground has been abandoned. In 1902, it recognized the legality of excluding negroes from local unions, central labor bodies, or federal labor unions; national unions which expressly exclude negroes are now affiliated with the Federation and, in 1902, the Stationary Engineers altered their by-laws so as to exclude negroes. At the Atlanta University conference on the negro artisan in 1902, a list was given of forty-four of the most important unions, several with a membership of over 30,000, which have not a single negro member. Obviously, in view of this drift in his organization, it is highly significant that while Mr. Gompers denies having advocated the *putting out* of negroes from unions, he does not deny having advocated their not being admitted.

To those who do not believe in the unionization of all laboring men, who, while admitting the benefits gained by organization, feel that there ought always to be a large body of free labor to offset the evils of the unions, this attitude of the Federation and its leader will give some satisfaction. Excluding the negroes means that there will be a steadily growing body of skilled and unskilled laborers available for those who wish to employ non-union labor. For Mr. Gompers and his workmen, in the long run, the proper policy is to admit negroes and to ask for them the education which, in many sections, is virtually denied them.

~ 1923 ~

Jim Crow in Texas

William Pickens

William Pickens was the author of several books on race,
including *Bursting Bonds* (1923) and *American Aesop* (1969).

August 15, 1923 ~ The classics tell us about the tortures invented by the
Sicilian tyrants, but the Sicilian genius for cruelty was far inferior to that of
the fellow who contrived the Jim Crow car system to harass the colored
population of the South. There are tens of thousands of white people in this
country who would be uncompromisingly opposed to this exquisite torture
if they only understood it. But *they* are not "jim crowed," they have not the
experience, and they do not and almost *cannot* understand what the colored
brother finds to complain of. Have you noticed how difficult it is to explain
a sensation or a pain to someone who never experienced it?

Fourteen states have Jim Crow car laws. Not one of them maintains
"equal accommodations" for colored people, although the law generally
calls for accommodations "equal in all points of service and convenience,"
so as to square with the Fifteenth Amendment. Nobody expects the railroads to go to the expense of duplicating their accommodations for the
colored, non-voting, minority population. The result is that the colored
traffic is usually attached to the general service with the least possible
expense: a small waiting-room in one corner of the station, generally
unswept and otherwise uncared-for; a compartment in one end of the
white men's smoker for all the colored people—men, women, and children—to ride in; generally no wash basin and only one toilet for both
sexes; with no privilege of taking meals in the diner or buying a berth in a
sleeper. Colored passengers taking a journey of several days must either
carry cold food enough to last or else buy the high-priced trash of the
newsboy. A colored woman traveling three nights from El Paso, Texas, to
Charleston., S.C., with a baby and small children, is compelled to carry
cold food and to sit up on straight-backed seats for the whole trip. A colored
woman of Portland, Oregon, editor of a paper there, bright, intelligent,
and attractive, respected by the best-known white and colored people of
the state, was visiting her parents in Texas, carrying her infant and a small
child of three years. On their third night's ride, in Texas, she was com-

pelled to get up, dress herself and babies, and vacate her berth because some short-distance white passengers objected to her presence in the car. A colored person who was hurrying from Florida to undergo an operation by an expert in Chicago had to risk death by a twenty-four-hour ride in a Jim Crow day coach. Sick colored people sometimes have to be carried on stretchers in the baggage car.

I sit in a Jim Crow as I write, between El Paso and San Antonio, Texas. The Jim Crow car is not an institution merely to "separate the races"; it is a contrivance to humiliate and harass the colored people and so torture them with a finesse unequaled by the cruelest genius of the heathen world. The cruder genius broke the bodies of individuals occasionally, but Jim Crow tortures the bodies and souls of tens of thousands hourly.

In the last two months I have ridden many thousands of miles in comfortable Pullman reservations out from New York to the great Northwest, with many stops and side trips; then down from Tacoma and past the Golden Gate to the City of the Angels, from the red apples of Spokane to the golden apples of the southwestern Hesperides; and then on by the petrified forest, the great canyon, and through the ancient cliff-dwellings of man to Albuquerque, New Mexico. In Albuquerque I had bought my reservation to El Paso, Texas. El Paso is where the train would enter Texas, and both my tickets terminated there. But so thoroughly is it understood that Jim Crowism is not designed merely to "separate," but also to humiliate, colored passengers that the thing is always in the consciousness of the railway employees, even those who operate in and out of Jim Crow territory, and they begin to "work on you" as soon as you buy a ticket that leads even to the limbo of this hell.

"Well, you can't ride in this car after you get into Texas. You'll have to get out of this car in Texas, and I suppose you know that?" This from the Pullman conductor, in a very gruff and loud voice, so that the whole car might hear him, while he and others stare and glare upon me. His speech is absolutely unnecessary since my tickets call only for El Paso, but the object is to "rub it in." I answered with not a word nor a look, save such mild and indifferent observation as I might bestow upon idiots who should spit at me or lick out their tongues as I passed by their cells of confinement.

In El Paso, because of the miscarriage of a telegram, my friends did not meet the train and I had to call them up and wait till they came down. I was meanwhile shown to the "Negro" waiting-room, a space of about twenty by twenty, away off in one corner of the station structure like a place of quarantine or a veritable hole in the wall. I had to traverse the entire length of the great main waiting-room in order to reach this hole. This main waiting-room has all the conveniences, 'phone booths, ticket offices, and whatnot. And whom do you suppose I saw in this main waiting-room as I passed through? Not only the "white people," but all the non-American "colored peoples," yellow Chinese, brown Japanese, and the many-colored Mexicans, some dirty with red handkerchiefs around their necks and carrying baskets and bundles with fruits, vegetables, and live chickens. These Mexicans are the people whom the colored soldiers of the Twenty-fourth Infantry held off those white people some years ago. And if we should go to war with Japan the colored American will again be expected to rush forth from that hole in the wall to the defense of his white compatriot. I say all this without the slightest feeling of animosity toward any race, and absolutely without scorn of any human misfortune. I am only stating the case plainly. And when I reached the little humiliating hole assigned to "Negroes," I found there only four or five colored people, all intelligent, not one of them conspicuously unkempt like some of the Mexicans in the main waiting-room. Those Mexicans were being treated as human beings, as they should be treated. These colored people knew that this arrangement was not so much for their separation as for their humiliation and attempted degradation, and it formed the burden of their conversation.

I stayed in El Paso two nights and three days. Its colored people are alert to the situation. By means of their automobiles they protected me against the "rear-seat" treatment of the electric street cars. They took me across the shallow Rio Grande into Mexico, just a few hundred yards from Jim Crowism. And over there, bless you, white and black people come out of Texas and gamble at the same table, drink at the same bar, and eat in the same restaurant, while the dark and almost black Mexican stands around as the policeman and the law.

Then I went to buy a ticket for San Antonio. I did not expect to buy a Pullman ticket, but I did expect to buy a day coach ticket on any train. But I found that colored passengers are allowed to go to San Antonio on but one train a day, the one that leaves at night. The morning train carried only Pullmans, and colored folk are made to wait twelve hours longer for the train that carries a Jim Crow compartment. A colored man's mother may be dying in San Antonio, but he must wait. Any Mexican, however, who the colored infantry fought on the border and did not happen to kill, can ride on any train. Any foreigner, or any foreign spy who happens to be loose in the land, can travel freely, but not the mothers or wives or sisters of the black Americans who fought, bled, and died in France. All the rest of the world, be he an unlettered Mexican peon, an untrammeled Indian, or a representative of the uncivilized "white trash" of the South, can get either train; but the Negro, be he graduate of Harvard or bishop of the church, can go only once daily.

In the Jim Crow car there was but one toilet and wash-room, for use of colored women and men. And the Jim Crow car is not a car, mind you, but only the end of a car, part of the white men's smoker, separated from the white smokers only by a partition that rises part of the way from the floor toward the ceiling, so that all the sickening smoke can drift over all night and all day. And yet what do you suppose the colored porter said as he swept out the Jim Crow end this morning? Nobody asked him, he volunteered as he swept: "Well, this is the cleanest floor I have to sweep every morning. Them white folks and Mexicans and things back yonder sho' do mess up the floors!"

When I reached the dining-car there was not another person there. I was asked did I "want anything." I replied briefly, breakfast. Then there was confusion and much conferring between the steward and several colored waiters at the other end of the car. The steward kept glancing at me meanwhile, as if endeavoring to "size me." Finally I was given a seat at the end of the car where the porters eat. Oatmeal, eggs, and postum were brought, and then a green curtain was drawn between me and the rest of the vacant dining-car! Remember, this did not all happen in some insane asylum, but in Texas. The check on which I was to order my food was a green check, a "porter's check," so that I should not need to be treated to such little formalities as an extra plate or a finger bowl. I deliberately wrote my name down in the blank for "porter," but I was charged a passenger's fare. It all meant that I would not eat any more that day, although I was not to reach San Antonio till eight or nine at night.

One must be an idiot not to comprehend the meaning and the aim of these arrangements. There is no such thing as a fair and just Jim Crow system with "equal accommodations," and in very human nature there will never be. The inspiration of Jim Crow is a feeling of caste and a desire to "keep in its place," that is, to degrade, the weaker group. For there is no more reason for a Jim Crow car in public travel than there would be for a Jim Crow path in the public streets. Those honest-souled, innocent-minded people who do not know, but who think that the Jim Crow system of the South is a bona fide effort to preserve mere racial integrity on a plane of justice are grievously misled. Any man should be permitted to shut out whom he desires from his private preserves, but justice and Jim Crowism in public places and institutions are as far apart and as impossible of union as God and Mammon.

~ 1 9 2 5 ~

Georgia: Invisible Empire State

W.E.B. Du Bois

The sociologist, educator, author and activist W.E.B. Du Bois
led the shift away from Booker T. Washington's accommoda-
tionist strategy by founding the more militant Niagara
Movement in 1905. He also co-founded the N.A.A.C.P. and
edited its journal, *Crisis*, from 1909 to 1932. Du Bois contributed this piece to *The Nation*'s long-running series "These
United States."

JANUARY 21, 1925 ~ Georgia is beautiful. High on the crests of the Great
Smoky Mountains some Almighty Hand shook out this wide and silken
shawl—shook it and swung it two hundred glistening miles from the
Savannah to the Chattahoochee, four hundred miles from the Appala-
chians to the Southern sea. Red, white, and black is the soil and it rolls by
six great rivers and ten wide cities and a thousand towns, thick-throated,
straggling, low, busy, and sleepy. It is a land singularly full of lovely
things: its vari-colored soil, its mighty oaks and pines, its cotton-fields, its
fruit, its hills.

And yet few speak of the beauty of Georgia. Some tourists wait by the
palms of Savannah or try the mild winters of Augusta; and there are those
who, rushing through the town on its many railroads, glance at Atlanta or
attend a convention there. Lovers of the mountains of Tennessee may skirt
the mountains of Georgia; but Georgia connotes to most men national
supremacy in cotton and lynching, Southern supremacy in finance and
industry, and the Ku Klux Klan.

Now, all this is perfectly logical and natural. Georgia does not belong
to this nation by history or present deed. It is a spiritual borderland lying
in the shadows between Virginia and Carolina on the one hand,
Louisiana on the other, and the great North on the last. It is a land born
to freedom from a jail delivery of the unfortunate, which insisted pas-
sionately upon slavery and gave poor old Oglethorpe and the London
proprietors many a bad night because they tried to prohibit rum and
slaves. But Georgia was firm and insisted: "In Spight of all Endeavours to
disguise this Point, it is as clear as Light itself, that Negroes are as essen-

tially necessary to the Cultivation of Georgia, as Axes, Hoes, or any other Utensil of Agriculture."

When catastrophe came, Georgia was among the first to see a way out. While other states were seeking two impossible and incompatible things, the subjection of the blacks and defiance of the North, Georgia developed a method of her own. With slavery gone the slave baron was bankrupt and two heirs to his power had rushed forward: The poor white from the hills around and above Atlanta and the Northern speculator—"Scalawag" and "Carpet-Bagger" they were dubbed—sought to rebuild the South. In the more purely agricultural regions this involved a mere substitution of owners and black laborers. But the development of Georgia was to be more than agricultural. It was to be manufacturing and mining; transportation, commerce, and finance; and it was to involve both white and colored labor. This was a difficult and delicate task, but there were Georgians who foresaw the way long before the nation realized it. The first prophet of the new day was Henry W. Grady of Atlanta.

Grady's statue stands in Atlanta in the thick of traffic, ugly, dirty, but strong and solid. He had Irish wit, Southern fire, and the flowers of oratory. He was among the first to incarnate the "Black Mammy" and he spoke in three years three pregnant sentences: in New York in 1886 he made a speech on the "New South" that made him and the phrase famous. He said: "There was a South of slavery and secession. That South is dead." The North applauded wildly. In Augusta, in 1887, he added: "In her industrial growth the South is daily making new friends. Every dollar of Northern money invested in the South gives us a new friend in that section." The South looked North for capital and advertised her industrial possibilities. And finally he said frankly in Boston in 1889: "When will the black man cast a free ballot? When the Northern laborer casts a vote uninfluenced by his employer."

In other words, Grady said to Northern capital: Come South and make enormous profits; and to Southern captains of industry: Attract Northern capital by making profit possible. Together these two classes were to unite and exploit the South; and they were to make Georgia not simply an industrial center but what was much more profitable, a center for financing Southern enterprises; and they would furnish industry with labor that could be depended on.

This last point, dependable labor, was the great thing. Here was a vast submerged class, the like or equivalent of which was unknown in the North. Here were a half-million brawny Negro workers and a half-million poor whites. If they could be kept submerged—hard at work in industry and agriculture—they would raise cotton, make cotton cloth, do any number of other valuable things, and build a "prosperous" state. If they joined forces, and went into politics to better their common lot, they would speedily emancipate themselves. How was this to be obviated? How were both sets of laborers to be inspired to work hard and continuously? The *modus operandi* was worked out slowly but it was done skillfully, and it brought results. These results have been costly, but they have made Georgia a rich land growing daily richer. The new wealth was most unevenly distributed; it piled itself in certain quarters and particularly in Atlanta—birthplace and capital of the new "Invisible Empire."

The method used to accomplish all this was, in addition to much thrift and hard work, deliberately to encourage race hatred between the mass of white people and the mass of Negroes. This was easy to develop because the two were thrown into economic competition in brick-laying, carpentry, all kinds of mechanical work connected with the new industries. In such work Negroes and whites were personal, face-to-face competitors, bidding for the same jobs, working or willing to work in the same places. The Negroes started with certain advantages. They were the mechanics of the period before the war. The whites came with one tremendous advantage, the power to vote. I remember a campaign in Atlanta. The defeated candidate's fate was sealed by a small circular. It contained a picture of colored carpenters building his house.

Hoke Smith in his memorable campaign in Georgia in 1906 almost repeated Stephens of forty-five years earlier:

I believe the wise course is to plant ourselves squarely upon the proposition in Georgia that the Negro is in no respect the equal of the white man, and that he cannot in the future in this State occupy a position of equality.

A white labor leader, secretary of the Brotherhood of Timber Workers, wrote about the same time:

The next cry raised by the bosses and their stool pigeons is the "Negro question," and so we are often asked, How will the brotherhood handle the Negro and the white men in the same organization? Answer: How do the capitalists or employers handle them? To the employer a workingman is nothing but a profit-producing animal and he doesn't care a snap of his finger what the animal's color is— white, black, red, brown, or yellow; native or foreign born; religious or unreligious—so long as he (the worker) has strength enough to keep the logs coming and the lumber going—that is all the bosses want or ask. It is only when they see the slaves uniting, when all other efforts to divide the workers on the job have failed, that we hear a howl go up as to the horrors of "social equality." Not until then do we really know how sacred to the boss and his hirelings is the holy doctrine of "white supremacy."

On the other hand, once the laborers are thrown into hating, fearing, despising, competing groups, the employers are at rest. As one firm said in

1901, comparing its black labor with white: "Do the same work, and obey better; more profit, less trouble."

In agriculture poor whites and Negroes were soon brought into another sort of indirect competition. The Negroes worked in the fields, the poor whites in the towns which were the market-places for the fields. Gradually the poor whites became not simply the mechanics but the small storekeepers. They financed the plantations and fleeced the workers. They organized to keep the workers "in their places," to keep them from running away, to keep them from striking, to keep their wages down, to terrorize them with mobs. On the other hand the Negroes worked to own land, to escape from country to city, to cheat the merchants, to cheat the landholders.

Then in larger ways and more indirectly both groups of workers came into competition. They became separated according to different, but supporting and interlocked, industries and occupations. Negroes prepared the road-bed for the railroads; whites were engineers. Negroes were firemen; whites were engineers. Negroes were porters; whites were mill operatives. Finally there was the Negro servant stretching all the way from the great mansion to the white factory hand's hovel, touching white life at every point.

Soon the subtle rivalry of races in industry began. Soon, to the ordinary Georgia white man, the Negro became a person trying to take away his job, personally degrade him, and shame him in the eyes of his fellows; starve him secretly. To the ordinary Georgia Negro, the average white man was a person trying to take away his job, starve him, degrade him, keep him in ignorance, and return him to slavery. And these two attitudes did not spring from careful reasoning. They were so coiled and hidden with old known and half-known facts that they became matters of instinct and inheritance. You could not argue about them; you could not give or extract information.

It is usual for the stranger in Georgia to think of race prejudices and race hatred as being the great, the central, the unalterable fact and to go off into general considerations as to race differences and the eternal likes and dislikes of mankind. But that line leads one astray. The central thing is not race hatred in Georgia; it is successful industry and commercial investment in race hatred for the purpose of profit.

Skillfully, but with extraordinary ease, the power to strike was gradually taken from both white and black labor. First the white labor vote was used to disenfranchise Negroes and the threat of white competition backed by the hovering terror of the white mob made a strike of black workers on any scale absolutely unheard of in Georgia. Continually this disenfranchisement went beyond politics into industry and civil life. On the other hand, the power of a mass of cheap black labor to underbid almost any class of white laborers forced white labor to moderate its demands to the minimum and to attempt organization slowly and effectively only in occupations where Negro competition was least, as in the cotton mills.

Then followed the curious and paradoxical semi-disenfranchisement of white labor by means of the "white primary." By agreeing to vote on one issue, the Negro, the normal split of the white vote on other questions or the development of a popular movement against capital and privilege is virtually forestalled. Thus in Georgia democratic government and real political life have disappeared. None of the great questions that agitate the nation—international or national, social or economic—can come up for free discussion. Anything that would divide white folk in opinion or action is taboo and only personal feuds survive as the issues of political campaigns. If real issues ever creep in and real difference of opinion appears— "To Your Tents, O Israel"—Do you want your sister to marry a "nigger"?

What induces white labor to place so low a value on its own freedom and true well-being and so high a value on race hatred? The answer involves certain psychological subtleties and yet it is fairly clear. The Southern white laborer gets low wages measured in food, clothes, shelter, and the education of his children. But in one respect he gets high pay and that is in the shape of the subtlest form of human flattery—social superiority over masses of other human beings. Georgia bribes its white labor by giving it public badges of superiority. The Jim Crow legislation was not to brand the Negro as inferior and to separate the races, but rather to flatter white labor to accept public testimony of its superiority instead of higher wages and social legislation. This fiction of superiority invaded public affairs: No Negro schoolhouse must approach in beauty and efficiency a white school; no public competition must admit Negroes as competitors; no municipal improvements must invade the Negro quarters until every white quarter approached perfection or until typhoid threatened the whites; in no city and state affairs could Negroes be recognized as citizens—it was Georgia, Atlanta, the Fourth Ward, *and* the Negroes.

In return for this empty and dangerous social bribery the white laborer fared badly. Of modern social legislation he got almost nothing; the "age of consent" for girls in Georgia was ten years until 1918, when it was, by great effort and outside pressure, raised to fourteen. Child labor has few effective limitations; children of twelve may work in factories and without birth registration the age is ascertainable with great difficulty. For persons "under twenty-one" the legal workday is still "from sunrise to sunset," and recently Georgia made itself the first state in the Union to reject the proposed federal child-labor amendment. Education is improving, but still the white people of Georgia are one of the most ignorant groups in the Union and the so-called compulsory education law is so full of loopholes as to be unenforceable. And black Georgia? In Atlanta there are twelve thousand Negro children in school and six thousand seats in the schoolrooms! In all legislation tending to limit profits and curb the exploitation of labor Georgia lingers far behind the nation.

This effort to keep the white group solid led directly to mob law. Every white man became a recognized official to keep Negroes "in their places." Negro baiting and even lynching became a form of amusement which the authorities dared not stop. Blood-lust grew by what it fed on. These outbreaks undoubtedly affected profits, but they could not be suppressed, for they kept certain classes of white labor busy and entertained. Secret government and manipulation ensued. Secret societies guided the state and administration. The Ku Klux Klan was quite naturally reborn in Georgia and in Atlanta.

Georgia is beautiful. Yet on its beauty rests something disturbing and strange. Physically this is a certain emptiness and monotony, a slumberous, vague dilapidation, a repetition, an unrestraint. Point by point one could pick a poignant beauty—one golden river, one rolling hill, one forest of oaks and pines, one Bull Street. But there is curious and meaningless repetition until the beauty palls or fails of understanding. And on this physical strangeness, unsatisfaction, drops a spiritual gloom. There lies a certain brooding on the land—there is something furtive, uncanny, at times almost a horror. Some folk it so grips that they never see the beauty—the hills to them are haunts of grim and terrible men; the world goes armed with loaded pistols on the hip; concealed, but ready—always ready. There is a certain secrecy about this world. Nobody seems wholly frank—neither white nor black; neither child, woman, nor man. Strangers ask each other pointed searching questions: "What is your name?" "Where are you going?" "What might be your business?" And they eye you speculatively. Once satisfied, the response is disconcertingly quick. They strip their souls naked before you; there is sudden friendship and lavish hospitality. And yet—yet behind all are the grim bars and barriers; subjects that must not be touched, opinions that must not be questioned. Side by side with that warm human quality called "Southern" stands the grim fact that right here and beside you, laughing easily with you and shaking your hand cordially, are men who hunt men: who hunt and kill in packs, at odds of a hundred to one under cover of night. They have lynched five hundred Negroes in forty years; they have killed unnumbered white men. There must be living and breathing in Georgia today at least ten thousand men who have taken human life, and ten times that number who have connived at it.

Nevertheless, there are brave men in Georgia, men and women whose souls are hurt even to death by this merciless and ruthless exploitation of race hatred. But what can they do? It is fairly easy to be a reformer in New York or Boston or Chicago. One can fight there for convictions, and while it costs to oppose power, yet it can be done. It even gains some applause and worthwhile friends. But in Atlanta? The students of white Emory College recently invited a student of black Morehouse College to lead a Y.M.C.A. meeting. It was a little thing—almost insignificant. But in Georgia it was almost epoch-making. Ten years ago it would have meant riot. Today it called for rare courage. When the Southern Baptists met in Atlanta recently they did not segregate Negro visitors. Such a thing has seldom if ever happened before in Georgia. It is precisely the comparative insignificance of these little things that shows the huge horror of the bitter fight between Georgia and civilization.

Some little things a liberal public opinion in Georgia may start to do, although the politico-economic alliance stands like a rock wall in the path of real reform. A determined group called "inter-racial" asks for change. Most of them would mean by this the stopping of lynching and mobbing, decent wages, abolition of personal insult based on color. Most of them would not think of demanding the ballot for blacks or the abolition of Jim Crow cars or civil rights in parks, libraries, and theaters or the right of a man to invite his black friend to dinner. Some there are who in their souls would dare all this, but they may not whisper it aloud—it would spoil everything; it would end their crusade. Few of these reformers yet fully envisage the economic nexus, the real enemy encased in enormous profit. They think reform will come by right thinking, by religion, by higher culture, and do not realize that none of these will work its end effectively as long as it pays to exalt and maintain race prejudice.

Of the spiritual dilemmas that face men today I know of none more baffling than that which faces the conscientious, educated, forward-looking white man of Georgia. On the one hand is natural loyalty to what his fathers believed, to what his friends never question; then his own difficulty in knowing or understanding the black world and his inbred distrust of its ability and real wish; there is his natural faith in his own ability and the ability of his race; there is the subtle and continuous propaganda—gossip, newspapers, books, sermons, and "science"; there is his eager desire to see his section take a proud place in the civilized world. There is his job, his one party, his white primary—his social status so easily lost if he is once dubbed a "nigger lover." Facing all this is lynching, mob murder, ignorance, silly self-praise of people pitifully degenerate in so many cases, exploitation of the poor and weak, and insult, insult, insult heaped on the blacks.

Open revolt comes now and then. Once Tom Watson tried to unite labor. He organized the Populist Party in Georgia and invited the blacks to help. It was a critical situation that developed in the early nineties, when it was increasingly difficult to keep the Negro disfranchised illegally and not yet possible to disenfranchise him legally. In the first campaign it was easy to beat the Populists by the fraud of "counting them out." Immediately thereafter the captains of industry mobilized. By newspaper, by word of mouth, by lodge communications it was conveyed to the white workers that not only would Negroes benefit from any attempt to better the present industrial situation, but they would gradually displace the white workers by underbidding them; that any benefits for white workers must come secretly and in such a way that Negroes could not share in the benefits. Thus immediately the emphasis was put on race discrimination. And this race difference grew and expanded until in most cases the whole knowledge and thought of the workers and voters went to keeping Negroes down, rather than to raising themselves.

Internal dissension in the labor ranks followed. The Negroes were then blamed for not voting solidly with white labor, for selling out to capital, for underbidding labor. The whole movement swung into intense Negro hatred; and the net result was that the white labor vote turned eventually into a movement finally and completely to disenfranchise Negro labor. The mob shot down Watson's Negro leaders in their tracks and the only way in which he could survive politically was to out-Herod Herod in his diatribes against Negroes and in coining new variants of appeals to prejudice by attacks on Catholics and Jews. To his death he kept a dangerous political power and even reached the United States Senate, but with his labor party cut in two and forced into additional disenfranchisement by the "white primary" he could not menace the "machine."

The minds of the mob must be turned again and turned from political and economic thought to pure race hatred. Immediately the sex motif arose to leadership. All subconsciously, sex hovers about race in Georgia. Every negro question at times becomes a matter of sex. Voting? They want social equality. Schools? They are after our daughters. Land? They'll rape our wives. Continually the secrecy, the veiled suggestion, the open warning pivot on sex; gossip rages and horrible stories are spread. So it was at the culmination of the Hoke Smith campaign. All restraint was suddenly swept away and submerged in wild stories of rape and murder. Atlanta papers rushed out extra editions each with a new horror afterward proved wholly fictitious or crassly exaggerated. On a Saturday night the white Atlanta laborers arose and murdered every Negro they could catch in the streets. For three days war and rapine raged—then the streets of the Empire City sank into awful silence. Hoke Smith became Governor and Senator, and the industrial and political systems were intact.

All these occasions of revolt against the present political and industrial situation have thus ignored the Negro as an active factor in the revolution. But he cannot be ignored. In truth there can be no successful economic change in Georgia without the black man's cooperation. First of all the Negroes are property holders. Sixty years after slavery and despite everything Georgia Negroes own two million acres of land, a space nearly as large as the late kingdom of Montenegro. Their taxable property saved from low wages and systematic cheating has struggled up from twelve million dollars in 1890 to over sixty million today; and now and then even the remnant of their political power strikes a blow. In 1923 in Savannah a fight within the "white primary" between the corrupt gang and decency gave twelve hundred Negro voters the balance of power. Efforts were made to intimidate the Negroes. Skull and crossbones signed by the Ku Klux Klan were posted on the doors of eight of the prominent Negro churches with the legend, "This is a white man's fight; keep away." Warning slips were put under the doors of colored citizens. In vain. The colored voters held their own political meetings, financed their own campaign, went into the election, and of their twelve hundred votes it was estimated that less than a hundred went for the gang; the reform mayor was elected.

I am in the hot, crowded, and dirty Jim Crow car, where I belong. A black woman with endless babies is faring forth from Georgia, "North." Two of the babies are sitting on parts of me. I am not comfortable. Then I look out of the window. The hills twist and pass. Slowly the climate changes—cold pines replace the yellow monarchs of the South. There is no cotton. From the door of hewn log cabins faces appear—dead white faces and drawn, thin forms. Here live the remnants of the poor whites.

I look out of the window, and somehow it seems to me that here in the Jim Crow car and there in the mountain cabin lies the future of Georgia—in the intelligence and union of these laborers, white and black, on this soil wet with their blood and tears. They hate and despise each other today. They lynch and murder body and soul. They are separated by the width of a world. And yet—and yet, stranger things have happened under the sun than understanding between those who are born blind.

~ 1931 ~

The Black Bugs

Horace R. Cayton

Horace R. Cayton was a social scientist and author of several classic early studies of black urban life, including *Black Workers* (1939) and *Metropolis* (1945).

SEPTEMBER 9, 1931 ~ I sat eating in a small restaurant in the heart of the Black Belt of Chicago. As I finished my somewhat greasy steak and started on the "home-made apple pie," I chanced to look out the window and saw a number of Negroes walking by, three abreast, forming a long uninterrupted line.

On going outside I was informed that they were the "black bugs"—the Communists—the "black reds." Oh, so Mr. Fish and his calamity shouters were right. Indeed the Communists, it appeared, had been active with the black brethren. Here at last was a bit of concrete evidence that the fundamental institutions of the country were in danger. Here was evidence of the "red scare" which had kept many a corrupt municipal government, from New York to Seattle, in power a bit longer, and delayed grand jury investigations. I would accompany this band of black demons too, if not to protect our glorious institutions, at least to see them in part destroyed. I fell into line and marched.

Turning to my marching companion I asked where we were headed for, and what we would do when we got there. He looked surprised, and told me we were marching down to put in a family who had been evicted from a house for not paying their rent. Things were awfully tough down in the Black Belt now, he continued, and jobs were impossible to get. The Negro was the first to be discharged and the last to be hired. Now with unemployment they were hungry, and if they were put out in the street their situation would be a desperate one. The Negroes of the community had been exploited for years by the unscrupulous landlords who had taken advantage of prejudice compelling the Negroes to live only in that district, and had forced them to pay exorbitant rents. Now, continued my informer, hard times had hit them and they were being turned out into the street. Furthermore, as the Negroes did not know their legal rights, the landlords would simply pitch their few belongings out of the window with no legal procedure at all. They, the Communists, were going to see that the people were not treated in this fashion.

Need I say that my reaction was one of surprise and disappointment? Instead of trying to destroy our splendid and glorious institutions, these poor black folks were simply going over to put a fellow race member back into the house he had been unceremoniously kicked out of. This was indeed a comedown for one who had expected to witness the destruction of constitutional American principles, such as, for example, "due process of law."

Suddenly a shout went around that there was another family in the next street that had been put out, and the procession started in that direction. This time I was far in the front to see the fun. We were met at the street by two squad cars of police who asked us where we were going. The black crowd swarmed around the officers and their cars like a hive of bees around their queen. The officers jumped out of their cars and told the crowd to move on. No one moved. Everyone simply stood and stared at them. One officer lost his head and drew his gun, leveling it at the crowd.

Then a young fellow stepped out of the crowd and said, "You can't shoot all of us and I might as well die now as any time. All we want is to see that these people, our people, get back into their homes. We have no money, no jobs, and sometimes no food. We've got to live some place. We are just acting the way you or anyone else would act."

In the back of the crowd some one got up on a soap box and started to speak. It was an old, wild-eyed, haglike woman. The crowd turned and listened to her.

I have heard lots of radicals talk. I have attended the meetings of Anarchists, Socialists, I.W.W.s and Communists. I understand, more or less, the rituals of Karl Marx, Lenin, and the rest. I am familiar with the usual harangue of the "soap boxer"—but this was different. This woman was not talking about any economic principles; she was not talking about any empty theories, nor was she concerned with some abstract Utopia to be gained from the movement of the "lower classes." She was talking about bread, and jobs, and places to sleep in. It was the talk of a person who had awakened from a pleasant dream to find that reality was hard, cold, and cruel.

Then I realized that all these people had suddenly found themselves face to face with hard, cold reality. They were the people who a few years ago had migrated from the South, in wagons, in cars, in trains, even walking. They had migrated with songs and hymns on their lips—with prayers to the Almighty for deliverance. They had come to the North and had been welcomed. Ah, America's great pool of unskilled labor was tapped; they had been sent to help the war. But pretty soon the war was over. And, later still, the good times and prosperity were over. With hard times they had felt the pinch of poverty, and now they were virtually starving to death in the paradise of a few years ago.

Just then a siren was heard—the whisper went around—the riot squad was coming!

All of the spectators stepped back, and the active participants formed a small nucleus around the speaker—packed in tight—a solid black lump of people. Two young fellows stood holding the woman up on the soap box in the middle.

Then the riot squad turned into the street, four cars full of blue-coated officers and a patrol wagon. They jumped out before the cars came to a stop and charged down upon the crowd. Night sticks and "billies" played a tattoo on black heads. Clubs came down in a sickening rain of blows on the woolly head of one of the boys who was holding her up. Blood spurted from his mouth and nose. Finally she was pulled down. A tremor of nervousness ran through the crowd. Then someone turned and ran. In a minute the whole group was running like mad for cover. One of the officers shot twice at one of the boys who had been holding up the woman speaker. The boy stumbled, grabbed his thigh, but kept on running. The woman was struggling in the arms of two husky policemen. It was all over in a minute, and all that was left was the soap box and the struggling black woman. I turned and left. Tomorrow I will perhaps read in the paper that a "red riot" was stopped only with the intervention of a number of officers; that "red" agitation among the Negroes is on the increase; that Mr. Fish, Mr. Hearst, and Mr. Jimmie Walker were right—American institutions really are in danger.

~ 1943 ~

Capitol Notes

I.F. Stone

One of America's most celebrated and iconoclastic journalists, I.F. Stone served as *The Nation*'s Washington correspondent from 1941 to 1946. He went on to found the legendary *I.F. Stone's Weekly*, an independent newsletter of opinion, which he edited for nineteen years (1953–1971).

APRIL 10, 1943 ~ It takes a little while to catch on to the extent to which Washington is a Jim Crow town. Although the Negro press reaches 4,000,000 readers every week, its correspondents are barred from the House and Senate press galleries and from White House press conferences. The Washington correspondents, though as likable and pleasant a crowd as one can meet anywhere, are dominated in this respect by Southern mores. I came up against this myself the other day—if I may be forgiven a personal note—when I asked William H. Hastie to lunch. I'd never met the Judge before and wanted to talk with him of his experiences in the War Department, where he had served for two years as civilian aide to Secretary Stimson. Judge Hastie is a Negro, and on inquiry I found that the only place I could take a Negro to lunch was the Union Station. I strongly disliked the idea of being forced to take a man of his distinction to a counter in a railroad station, and asked his permission to invite him to be my guest at the National Press Club. Judge Hastie is not one of those members of a minority who, having achieved some position in the world, prefer to shut their eyes to the wrongs of their fellows rather than endanger that standing. He has picketed drugstores here which refused to hire Negroes, and he was as willing as I to run the risk of some possible embarrassment.

It seems that this was the first time in the history of the club that anyone had ever taken a Negro there to lunch. Elmer Davis was addressing a special luncheon in the auditorium that day; so we got a table before anyone seemed to realize what had happened. A moment after we were seated, a page told me I was wanted on the telephone. In the hall I found that this was a ruse. The manager asked me if that was a colored man with me. I said it was. He declared that we would not be served. I said that as a member of the club I insisted on service for my guest and went back to the table. There we sat unserved until two o'clock, when we left for a Chinese restaurant.

The Judge, besides being the least stuffy of individuals and a thoroughly swell guy, is at least as cultivated as some of the third-rate advertising men and fourth-rate politicians who belong to the club. He is a Harvard Law School graduate, dean of Howard University Law School, a former member of the federal judiciary in the Virgin Islands, and has just won the Spingarn medal for 1942.

Under the constitution of the club special meetings must be called on petition of twenty-five members. I managed to obtain nine signatures, and a diverse collection of arguments from well-meaning people who agreed with me but. . . . Some people think the punctilio governing a supposed "private club" more important than elementary considerations of human decency. I resigned from the club.

~ 1956 ~

Miracle in Alabama

Carey McWilliams

Carey McWilliams, editor of *The Nation* from 1955 to 1975, was best known for his trenchant books and articles on immigration, social history and social change movements.

MARCH 3, 1956 ~ The indictment of a hundred or more Negroes in Montgomery for leading a peaceful mass protest movement against segregated city buses places not them but the American nation on trial. Whether we have the courage or candor to acknowledge it, the fact is that the indictment calls into question every value—moral, political and constitutional—to which we so glibly pledge allegiance; here and now is a test which will determine the loyalty of the entire nation to its basic ideals and values.

Great issues are sometimes difficult to recognize. The issue in Montgomery is not whether this outrageous indictment will be upheld in the courts; one may safely assume that, ultimately, it will be set aside. Nor is it primarily a question of whether racial violence in some form or other will occur. This may or may not happen. Something far more important is at stake in Montgomery, "the cradle of the Confederacy." America is promises. At stake in Montgomery is the fidelity of every citizen to the promises which are America.

It is one thing to ask citizens to be patient in seeking a redress of grievances; it is something else again when the right to petition for a redress of grievances is itself denied. The Montgomery indictment strikes at this right; it is a crude attempt to intimidate an entire community. The Negroes of Montgomery are not asserting a narrow legal principle; they are proclaiming to the world their insistence on being regarded as members of the human race. The movement they have organized is peaceful. It is moral. It is constitutional. Not to support their modest proclamation is to repudiate one's birthright and heritage as an American.

What is happening in Montgomery is in the nature of a miracle, something that has never happened in the history of the South. A community which only a few years ago, like most Negro communities in the South, gave the appearance of being inert and apathetic, without structure or form, has, without any outside help or assistance, organized itself into a disciplined, articulate, superbly confident community. This transformation represents a fulfillment of the American dream, achieved in broad daylight, in the full but uncomprehending gaze of the nation and the world. Not the false American dream of two-tone classy sports cars, kitchens laden with gadgets and "little" $17,000 ranch houses (California-style) in the suburbs; but a realization of the real American dream of freedom and equality and the dignity and worth of every human being.

The South of the White Citizens Councils understands what has happened. It realizes full well that the Montgomery bus boycott is a major historic development with irreversible consequences. If the Negroes win, the same non-violent Gandhian resistance may spread throughout the South. Hence the "white" South is determined to suppress it. At first the opposition could not believe the boycott would be sustained. Now an effort is being made to intimidate the leadership. Should intimidation fail, physical violence and terror may be used. Violence, in fact, has already been used. Yet the South should have the wit to recognize that the Montgomery Negroes cannot fail for the simple reason that they have already succeeded. Knowledge once given, we have been told, cannot be recalled. By indicting the leadership of this movement, the "white" South has—most ironically—not only advertised the methods used; it has acknowledged their effectiveness. Win or lose in Montgomery, this type of resistance is likely to spread.

The miracle in Alabama, unheralded, without precedent, has put the entire nation to the test. It is not merely that the Administration from the President down has been placed on notice that the lives and liberties of the Negro residents of Montgomery are endangered; this they have been told. The test is much broader. It is addressed to the trade unions, the churches, press, veterans groups, civic organizations—to the entire nation. It is addressed with peculiar directness to American Protestantism. The twenty-six Negro ministers who are identified with this movement have given their brethren an example of Christian social leadership that is truly inspiring. "If we are arrested every day," the Reverend Martin Luther King Jr.—the name has a fine echo—told his fellow walkers, "if we are exploited every day, let nobody pull you so low as to hate them. We must use the weapon of love. We must have compassion and understanding for those who hate us. So many people have been taught to hate, taught from the cradle. They are not totally responsible."

As witnesses to this magnificent demonstration, we cannot stand around, in John Jay Chapman's phrase, "like blighted things, like ghosts about Acheron, waiting for someone or something to determine" our destiny for us. If this dramatic demonstration of the potency of the American dream does not strike a response in the nation's conscience, then that dream has been corrupted. But what is happening in Montgomery is the most convincing proof that such is not the case. For here, in the heart of the "black belt" of the South, new hope and confidence and, above all, a new democratic leadership has emerged. An entire community has experienced a rebirth of freedom. The men and women who compose it now stand erect. Unafraid, in high spirits, without malice, they are walking with chants and prayers toward freedom's future in response to the American promise.

~ 1961 ~
The Historic Image
[Editorial]

In the heat of the Cold War and civil rights movement, *The Nation* took stock of America's image problem in an unsigned editorial.

June 3, 1961~ The press has become preoccupied with "the American Image" to the point that it has become a minor mania. Editorial writers solemnly—even lugubriously—tell us that in Alabama "the United States has lost another battle in the global cold war" *(The New York Times)* or "Anti-Negro riots in Alabama cast a long and darkening shadow over American policy" (New York *Herald Tribune).* Mr. Lippmann, normally a confident and sanguine man, speaks of "the tragedy of Alabama," and even the Birmingham *News,* which last year publicly chastised Harrison Salisbury for having said in *The New York Times* that "fear and hatred" stalked the streets of Birmingham, now voices its own deep concern over Alabama's and America's image.

The Nation does not share this masochistic mood. We do not shudder, much less collapse, when informed that harsh things have been said about Alabama, U.S.A., by Radio Moscow, the *Giornale d'Italia* in Rome, *Nachtausgabe* in West Germany, the *Ethiopian Herald* of Addis Ababa, the *Ash Abah* of Tunisia, or, unkindest cut of all, by every daily in Lisbon.

The question is, with what image are we to be concerned? on whose face does the camera focus? who is being interviewed? what is the totality of the impression conveyed? No American need feel apologetic about such men as the Rev. Martin Luther King Jr., the Rev. Ralph Abernathy or the Rev. Fred Shuttlesworth. Has Addis Ababa or Lisbon, perhaps, come up with finer exemplars of democratic leadership? Who can fail to be impressed with the Negroes and whites who, besieged, spent the night in the old First Baptist Church in Montgomery, thereby writing a new and splendid chapter in the history of that historic city and proving, once again, that the church can be a mighty fortress of the Lord?

What is the matter with us? Do we want to buy glory and honor at bargain-basement prices? What American need feel apologetic about Diane

Nash, the twenty-two-year-old Negro girl, a Freedom Rider, who said: "We will not stop. There is only one outcome." Or young James Zwerg, a white youngster from Appleton, Wisconsin, who said from his hospital bed: "We are prepared to die. These beatings cannot deter us from our purpose. We want only equality and justice and we will get it." Or young John Lewis, a Negro boy, wearing a six-inch-square bandage on his head, who said: "We will go forward." Who with eyes to read, or at least to stare at TV newscasts—and a salute here to CBS for a fine documentary on Birmingham—can fail to be proud of the image that *these* Americans have projected? Let the camera focus on *them*.

A great deal has been said in the public prints in the last year about the need for national purposes, national goals, a sense of moral dedication. Yet when a large and growing group of young Americans, Negro and white, gives us a magnificent demonstration of purpose and dedication, we elect not to praise them but to wail about the mobs who beset them. Our image-makers should dry their crocodile tears. The Freedom Riders have given them something to cheer about—if only they had the wit to recognize the historic American image when it stares at them from the front pages of their daily papers.

~ 1965 ~

Watts: The Forgotten Slum

Carey McWilliams

Beginning in 1965, urban riots erupted across America, symptomatic of the nation's failure to address the poverty and discrimination which continued to fall disproportionately on blacks despite the gains of the civil rights movement. Carey McWilliams, editor of *The Nation* from 1955 to 1975 and an expert on his native Southern California, explored the root causes of the Watts riot.

AUGUST 30, 1965 ~ Thirty-one dead, over 700 injured, 2,200 under arrest, 1,000 fires, property damage of $200 million—such is the preliminary toll for the long weekend of rioting in the Watts area of Los Angeles. A feverish search for scapegoats is now under way and will no doubt continue through the 1966 gubernatorial campaign. High on the scapegoat list is the self-righteous Chief of Police who dismisses as a "canard" the charge that the Los Angeles police could ever be guilty of brutality; apparently Chief Parker doesn't watch television. Then there is Sam Yorty, the agile Mayor, playing political tricks as always; warned of the possibility of riots, he did nothing. The list is long and includes The Heat—a favorite scapegoat in all race-riot investigations—and Social Conditions. Here Watts qualifies on all counts: dropouts, delinquency, disease and dependency. But none of these social factors alone or in combination necessarily "cause" race riots; actually it is when conditions seem to be improving that the riots usually explode. Predictably the forthcoming investigation ordered by Governor Brown will stress the same tiresome clichés: police brutality, inadequate leadership, The Heat, slum conditions. All the while the truth about Watts is right there in front of people, in plain boldface type, for all to read; so simple that it is incredible. The hatred and violence of race riots is triggered by contempt, and of all forms of contempt the most intolerable is nonrecognition, the general unawareness that a minority is festering in squalor. Until the riots began, Watts had simply been forgotten by the encompassing "white" community.

A sizable Negro community began to develop in Mud Town, as Watts was then called, after 1916; the community later spread along Central Avenue with the influx of Negro migrants from the South which came after World War I. In the 1920s, Watts was a well-known slum—the unfailing butt of bad jokes by comedians on the Orpheum circuit. But it did exist; people knew about it. Arna Bontemps wrote a novel about it (*God Sends Sunday*, 1931), while Gilmore Millen wrote a novel about the rise of Central Avenue (*Sweet Man*, 1932). For the new residents of the 1920s and 1930s, Watts was a fact: perceived, studied (a bit) and understood (to some extent). But the big post–World War II migration and boom changed all that.

Today there are thousands of new residents who have never seen Watts. They may have driven through it or over it or around it but never to it, nor have they ever stopped there except to change a tire. Artfully isolated from the disagreeable the *haute bourgeoisie* of Brentwood, Bel-Air and Beverly Hills can shop, lunch and play games for years on end without seeing a Negro except as a domestic. The new middle class, living in jerry-built "lily white" subdivisions, each with its own shopping center, can honestly claim to be no more aware of Watts than the nice Germans were of Belsen.

Two brief camera shots suggest the reality of Watts. In one a large, calm-voiced Negro patiently explained to Governor Brown that the larger community was "always taking from Watts and not putting back"; why, he wanted to know, "do they do us like they do?" In another shot, a Negro told the Governor that the Negroes of Watts "know how other people live"; they watch television. They know, he said, how much the government is spending on "missiles and things like that." They could hardly *not* know, living in Southern California. Only last fall, shortly before the election, President Johnson reminded the Californians that the government pours more than $2 billion annually into the payrolls of the state's aerospace industries, most of it in Southern California. For a time the general boom provided a measure of upward mobility even for Negro residents and thereby stimulated still further Negro migration. But for the last year or so, new Negro migrants have found themselves increasingly bottled up in Watts with little immediate prospect of escape, while being bombarded day and night with images of affluence, and constantly tempted by the well-stocked shelves of the supermarkets. Even so, matters might have gone along as before, given a measure of insight and recognition and understanding. Neglect can be tolerated; discrimination can be endured; but the contempt of indifference inflames.

If Watts lives in history it will be as the scene of the riots and the home of the Towers. The three Watts Towers, which have drawn the praise of distinguished art critics, were built by Simon Rodia alone, unaided, at his own expense, over a period of thirty-three years. He built the towers out of "waste" which he had collected: broken tiles, dishes, bottles, over 70,000 sea shells, bottle caps and whatnot. The walled garden from which the towers rise is covered with multicolored mosaics or with imprints of tools, hands, corncobs and baskets. Out of this "waste" he built three structures of great beauty. He built them with no drawing-board designs, machine equipment or scaffolding: they were literally "built in the air." Rodia was born in Rome and came to this country when he was 12. A tile setter and telephone repairman, he settled in Watts and devoted most of his life to building the towers which, when completed in 1954, he gave to the city and his neighbors. "I wanted to do something for the United States," he said, "because there are nice people in this country." Whatever his reasons, the towers—and the towers alone—redeem to some extent the ugliness and hatefulness of Watts, the slum Los Angeles forgot. In 1959 Rodia left Watts, not to return: a man of his quaint old-world social attitudes obviously did not belong in jet-age Los Angeles. He was reluctant to say why. "If your mother dies and you have loved her very much," he said, "maybe you don't speak of her." On July 21 he died in Martinez—in Northern California—at the age of 90. It is fitting that he died away from Watts and before the riots.

~ 1968 ~

Beale Street and Points North: Memphis is Also America

Pat Watters

Pat Watters is the author of three books about the South, including *Down to Now: Reflections on the Southern Civil Rights Movement* (1971). He worked at the Southern Regional Council from 1963 to 1975.

April 22, 1968 ~ His movement, his life were Southern; but Memphis, where he died, symbolized more than the South. Its racial crisis of 1968 and its murderous failure were those of all America. Dr. Martin Luther King Jr. went there during the fifth week of a garbage workers' strike that had built into a civil rights movement and a dangerous crisis. The Memphis Negro community had not developed much of a civil rights movement during the early 1960s. So the movement that did come in 1968 capsuled into a few swift weeks the decade's history of white America's failure to respond to the nonviolence of Dr. King, and black America's recoil into despair and a violence of desperation.

The strike began on February 12 over a grievance of twenty-two sewer workers. Thirteen hundred Negroes, most of them garbage workers, walked out. Negro leaders, including most ministers, began rather routine support of the strike, and became increasingly incensed over the intransigence of the Mayor in negotiations, and the ineffectiveness of the City Council. On February 23, the Council evaded taking a public stand in favor of union recognition, and Negroes hastily organized a march on the downtown section in protest. City police in large numbers—Negroes said too large—accompanied the march. When some marchers laid hands on a police car that some claimed had run over a woman's foot, officers cut loose with mace up and down the line of nonviolent demonstrators, spraying it into faces at close range, using it as punishment rather than a deterrent.

The police action in Memphis, the affront to the leaders—to men of God and to the people—was the unifying factor. From then on Memphis had a movement, a peaceful but deeply indignant one.

The issues of the strike were broadened to a protest against general conditions for Negroes, not unlike those in cities across the land—police brutality, unfit housing, lack of jobs, low wages, discrimination in schools. These, as Dr. King later noted, were the new national issues of Negro protest, economic at base, the focal point of the Poor People's Campaign. But the main issue in Memphis was dignity. Again and again, preachers, union leaders and others demanded dignity, deplored the indignity of the misused mace, of the Mayor's paternalistic treatment of negotiators, his failure even to understand the symbolic importance of union recognition for men whose legacy was the powerlessness of plantation laborers.

The Negro ministers were in charge through the rest of the fateful campaign; the mood was close to that of the early civil rights struggle—nonviolent, firm but patient, willing to work within traditional institutions. And until the assassination of Dr. King, this was the predominant mood among Negroes in the South. No major riot had occurred in a Southern city. The adherents of black power waited in the wings in Memphis; as across the South since 1966, the mood of black power had hovered but not taken over.

Young militants told the ministers to try their nonviolence; they would wait and act only when it was apparent nonviolence would accomplish nothing. And the ministers passed on the threat of this to the whites with whom they vainly sought accommodation, the ministers speaking their own anger and indignation, saying how their faith in nonviolence was shaking, how they might eventually have to "go fishing," leaving the field to the young militants.

The impasse and growing tension of the strike continued for five weeks before Dr. King came in. One evidence of white support heartened the Negroes; white unions gave money and on one day 500 white union members marched in support of the strike. There was talk that the nucleus of a real coalition between labor rank and file and the Negro movement was at last at hand.

But except for the unusual (in the South, unprecedented) solidarity of labor, there was no meaningful action from any level of white leadership or society to resolve what all should have recognized as a deadly dangerous situation. One of the biggest businessmen said unionization of public employees had to be stopped before it spread to police and firemen. The City Council, recently reorganized to be more powerful, failed to support the strike even verbally.

It was into this impasse that Dr. King walked on March 28. As the march of at least 5,000 got under way nonviolently, some young people, probably no more than fifty, took to the sidewalks and broke store windows. Leaders stopped the march just before police ordered it ended. Dr. King was whisked away; police violence took over. It was probably not possible for officers to apprehend the window-breakers and allow the march to continue. But police, by most accounts, discriminated not at all between the vandals and the nonviolent in their clubbings and beatings. They shot and killed one youth, accused of looting, injured nearly sixty Negroes, and arrested 280. Four thousand National Guardsmen came in, and a nightly curfew was enforced. Network television routinely reported that no Negro could be on the streets without a reason. It sounded like South Africa.

Other national reaction was not unlike that of white Memphis. Almost uniformly, indeed almost as a conditioned reflex, the press emphasized the window-breaking rather than the weeks of white Memphis's failure, and stressed implications for violence in Dr. King's planned march on Washington. Not the Memphis *Press-Scimitar* or *Commercial Appeal* but *The New York Times* commented that the effect of Dr. King's Memphis march was to "solidify white sentiment against the strikers," and said: "Dr. King must by now realize that his descent on Washington is likely to prove even more counter-productive." Eugene Patterson, editor of *The Atlanta Constitution* and a member of the United States Commission on Civil Rights, wrote: "Dr. King offers the best hope of keeping the smoke now heating in the ghettos from springing into fire. But in trying to recall the riotous element to the banner of non-violence, the outbreak of violence becomes his failure—and his problem, as well as America's, and particularly the Negro's." Alongside his column was a cartoon showing a diminutive Dr. King in the hands of a Frankenstein monster labeled "Mob Fever."

The President of the United States, in his first reaction to Memphis, said: "I want to again assure you that the resources of your government stand behind local law enforcement agencies to the full extent of our constitutional authority. Mindless violence—destroying what we have all worked so hard to build—will never be tolerated in America." On the same pattern had been Johnson's lukewarm, if not antagonistic, response to the urgent report of his National Advisory Commission on Civil Disorders, and his withdrawal of opposition to a riot-control bill to punish interstate travelers who contribute to violence.

The outpouring of grief and guilt and bathos after the assassination, coming from such an officialdom, a press, a society, and coming so soon after the similar meaningless mourning of President Kennedy, has to be called obscene. The appropriate response would be action—in Memphis, a just settlement of the garbage strike; in Washington, all the white sympathizers joining in the Poor People's March; in Congress, a full, not token, program to meet the needs of poverty and to eliminate institutionalized racism. Ending the war in Vietnam would have to be a corollary, morally related action.

During a march of students of the Atlanta University complex the day after the assassination, a Negro youth looked up to see Atlanta Police Chief Herbert Jenkins, noted for his liberal influence in the Riot Commission, riding by. The young man pointed a finger at the chief, and said, "You're going to the pay the price for this." The chief said nothing. A Negro Atlantan in his car said sadly a few minutes later, "Do you know who that kid was? One of the nine who desegregated Atlanta schools back in 1961." An era had begun and ended in the South in the young man's history, with the beginning and end of the career of Dr. King, the two not unconnected.

~ 1983 ~
Black Power in the Age of Jackson
Andrew Kopkind

Andrew Kopkind, a *Nation* associate editor from 1983 until his death in 1994, wrote on political movements and popular culture for more than thirty years. Many of these writings are collected in *The Thirties Years' Wars: Dispatches and Diversions of a Radical Journalist, 1965–1994* (Verso). In this article Kopkind discusses the relationship between the media and Jesse Jackson, whom he accompanied on Jackson's 1984 presidential campaign.

NOVEMBER 26, 1983 ~ Black power is an engine that drives the great vehicles of social change in America. The Civil War and the civil rights movement, slave revolts and student sit-ins, Marcus Garvey's separatism and Malcolm X's nationalism: black people's epic struggle for equality and quest for identity create both the pretext and the context for national upheaval and transformation. It is a radical dynamic that pertains to America's peculiar racial history, and in each generation it produces unique politics and unexpected leaders. Suddenly, in this electoral season, the politics are presidential and the leader is Jesse Jackson.

The national media plaster Jackson's face on magazine covers, pull him in front of television cameras and tuck him into the most conventional categories of presidential candidacy. Even the press that can't stand (or understand) his politics makes Jackson into some kind of hero; *Newsweek*'s cover story includes "a Jackson album" of snapshots, showing the candidate in historic poses from college football field to victory night after Chicago's mayoral election last winter. Not since John F. Kennedy burst into celebrity a quarter-century ago has a political upstart so captivated the press and captured attention, space and even *Time*: "He can be fascinating and frightening, inspiring and irritating, charismatic and controversial."

Such effusions are accompanied by detailed analyses, often with charts, of the mathematical probabilities for Jackson's strategy to succeed in the primaries. Then come discussions of Jackson's stated or implied positions on what pundits take to be issues in the election: missiles, motherhood and the Palestine Liberation Organization, for three. Finally, Jackson albums usually include an extended essay by the resident philosopher on every black child's dream of becoming President of the United States.

The level of muddle, misinformation, wrong thinking and barely disguised racism in all the hoopla is extraordinary, if predictable. In listing Jackson's "downside," commentators invariably call him "ambitious," "egotistical," "opportunistic" and "driven," as if such qualities were rare among presidential candidates. Who could be more ambitious than John Glenn, more opportunistic than Walter Mondale, more frightening than Ronald Reagan, more irritating than Gary Hart? But somehow (we *know* how) Jackson is fair game for taunts and teases from the press, while lighter folks get off with more qualified criticisms.

By the same token, the Jackson campaign and the phenomenon of a black political power movement are consistently denigrated or trivialized. Many politicians see the surge of black activism as merely the latest minority bid for the spoils of office (and even that bespeaks a misreading of the history of ethnic politics); one leftish columnist said cynically, "The whole thing will end with Mondale making Jackson his Secretary of HUD, or something." I've heard it said that Jackson's purpose is to "keep the Democrats honest," an oxymoronic hope at best, or, along the same lines, to "revive the New Deal coalition," an improbable medical and political dream.

The cynics may have a point; they often do. The media may be able to frame the Jackson campaign in familiar terms of charisma, clout and the delegate count; those are the most comfortable clichés. Politicians may defang and defuse the frightening and explosive elements of the movement; that is their prerogative. But black politics in the Age of Jackson has a vastly different center of gravity, historical message and meaning. "It's all about power," Stoney Cooks, a longtime associate of Atlanta Mayor Andrew Young, told me recently. It's also about race, about class, about enfranchisement and disenfranchisement, and about the mechanisms of change in the country. The movement is not peripheral to those transforming struggles in the American epic; it is at the very heart of the upheaval. In the course of a few months everything has moved: the spirit is impatient, the mood is militant, the tempo is rising and the color is black.

The speed of change is unprecedented. At this time last year, black politicians and black politics were nearly invisible in white America. The decline of the old civil rights movement, the force of the white backlash to integration and affirmative action, and the rise of Reaganism had pushed black struggles into a memory hole. Only two years ago, Adam Clymer, a senior political analyst for *The New York Times*, surveyed the scene and discovered that "the political influence of blacks in America has fallen to its lowest level in two decades."

The gains blacks had made in employment, education and political office after passage of the various anti-discrimination acts of the 1960s proved to be limited, and by the end of the next decade many of the vectors of progress were reversed. A report issued this year by the Center for the Study of Social Policy, a liberal think tank, showed that the median income for blacks was only 56 percent of that for whites—virtually the same as it was in 1960. Even worse, 45 percent of all adult black males were unemployed in 1982—almost twice as many as in 1960, also a year of economic downturn. Politically, black officeholders are still a token presence, even in Southern states with large black populations. There are no blacks among the eighty-two members of Congress from the seven states of the Deep South, where the Voting Rights Act of 1965 was targeted. As Jesse Jackson says repeatedly in his stump speeches, "Eighteen years after the Voting Rights Act, only 1 percent of elected officials are black. At that rate, it will take us 198 years to achieve parity."

Social relations between blacks and whites had been similarly stymied, if they had not actually deteriorated, by the mid-1970s. Racist chic replaced radical chic (if the latter was ever anything more than a gonzo magazine headline); liberal guilt ebbed and liberal good will dissipated. Liberal malice, on the other hand, became socially legitimate and politically shrewd. New York's Mayor Ed Koch, who once marched for black equality in Dixie, runs from it like the plague in his own hometown, and there are other politicians like him. The elaborate coded vocabulary used to disguise their racist ethic fools none but the most gullible editorial writers. Black and white voters (and non-voters) know how to translate "death penalty," "victims' rights," "poverty pimps," "welfare cheats" and "special interests" when used in white political parlance. And they act accordingly on election day. All during the 1970s, whites voted for whites and many blacks didn't bother.

Things started changing a year ago. The black political movement arose from the cynicism, disillusionment and reaction of the last long years; indeed, the movement was fashioned by the despair of the decade following the demise of the civil rights campaigns. It appeared not only *after* that time of hopelessness, of rejection, of broken promises and false starts but *because* of the many failures. That is crucial for the movement, and for Jesse Jackson as well.

Both Jackson and the movement exploded into political prominence and media visibility during the Chicago mayoral campaign of Harold Washington. That contest became the pivotal event in the development of the new black consciousness, what Jackson calls the beginning of "a six-week drama around the [Washington] victory and a six-month trauma afterward." It was vastly different from other black electoral victories of the past fifteen years because it was won in direct opposition to—and at the expense of—white Democrats of the liberal persuasion.

Walter Mondale and Edward Kennedy, the diarchs of Democratic liberalism, came to Chicago to stump for Washington's opponents: Kennedy for incumbent Mayor Jane Byrne, Mondale for Richard M. Daley, son of the late cloutish mayor. They hardly took notice of Washington's presence or his point, which was that it was black people's "turn" to hold office. The white politicians simply assumed what all white Democrats have assumed since the New Deal: blacks would be satisfied with the leavings of liberal power—the trickle-down effects of welfare policies and expanded public employment programs. As it turned out, those assumptions were obsolete.

Mondale and Kennedy came to Chicago to beat Harold Washington, Jackson remarked to me one steamy morning late last summer in a van bouncing through backwater Mississippi on a voter registration weekend. "You couldn't pay them to do that again. Things have changed."

What happened in Chicago was the beginning of the process Jackson calls the "renegotiation" of the relationship between blacks and the Democratic Party. For half a century, the Democrats have in a sense contracted to provide for and protect blacks and others traditionally rejected by the American system. Blacks were to respond with votes, support, enthusiasm and, perhaps most important, moral legitimacy. "Black voting is always sort of a moral initiative," Jackson said in a speech not long ago.

As the contract has run its course through several renewals but no serious reconstructions, the Democrats have often tried to wriggle out of important clauses. Even the great New Dealer Franklin Roosevelt was lambasted by black leaders for his poor performance; many did not want to support his campaign for a third term. Kennedy fudged on civil rights until the movement overtook him; organizers of the 1963 March on Washington were so suspicious of his motives and wary of his rhetoric that they rejected his request to speak at the Lincoln Memorial.

Lyndon Johnson wanted to be remembered for saying "We shall overcome" at a joint session of Congress, but before that, as he prepared for his nomination at the 1964 Democratic convention, he ordered the destruction of the most important independent black political movement of that era, the Mississippi Freedom Democratic Party. It's a long and sad tale, but the upshot is that Johnson and Hubert Humphrey demanded that blacks give up any hope of independent political standing and submit to the priorities, needs and strategies of white Democratic leaders if they wanted anti-poverty and civil rights benefits.

Most whites forgot the Freedom Democrats' challenge soon after the convention. But black activists and political workers—including everyone I met at the heart of the Jackson campaign—remember it vividly. For them, it is the landmark event in the development of black power consciousness and its political expression.

Everything Jesse Jackson is saying this year about blacks in politics— "We want our share," "It's our turn," "Blacks will no longer be the Harlem Globetrotters of the Democratic Party"—was first shouted, in many of the same words, by young black civil rights workers and militants in the wake of the liberal "betrayal" of the Freedom Democrats. I heard the basic Jackson speech in 1966 in Mississippi, when the first cries of "black power" went up; in Lowndes County, Alabama, where members of the Student Nonviolent Coordinating Committee settled down to start the Black Panther Party; in Oakland, California, where other black youths were organizing a similar project in an urban ghetto.

In all those cases, black power politics was the specific response to Democratic failures to give organized blacks a share in the power and profits of political control. But as a slogan and an idea, black power is old hat. Why has it taken nearly two decades for it to find expression in mainstream politics?

Jackson told me that blacks had to develop a certain amount of "maturity" before they could assimilate black power concepts and act on them. That means, perhaps, that they had to hear Democratic promises, believe them and see them broken. In other words, they had to want the Great Society and see it destroyed by the Democrats' bureaucratic control in Washington and their war in Vietnam; they had to suffer the depredations of corporate conservatism under Nixon; they had to plead for a better deal from Carter and see that hope deferred by the exigencies of Democratic inflation-fighting and cold war–mongering, and they had to bear the brunt of Reaganism's ravages, unaided and hardly comforted by their Democratic protectors. It's no wonder that in Chicago, blacks refused en masse to follow Mondale and Kennedy and give their votes to the white establishment which had led them on and let them down so many times.

To follow the political logic of black power politics is easier than to chart its future. But to see what the result of renegotiation may mean, it is best to start with Jesse Jackson's concept of black voting as a moral initiative. That view is surely more than bluff and pride. Black political activity has a unique potential in the American electoral scheme as a strategy in the struggle for justice and equality. That is not to say black votes count for more than those of any other group, but the fact of racism and the history of black exclusion give black electoral movements a special spiritual force.

A corollary to the formulation of moral initiative is Jackson's notion, which he explained to a New York audience recently, that "most other groups ride on the coattail of black strategy." That is not an altogether endearing insight: scores of self-perceived or self-constructed voting communities pretend to pre-eminence, not to mention political leadership. Whites of all stripes have historically ignored blacks and dismissed race as irrelevant or dangerous in political organization. Leftists sometimes call race mere "superstructure" over a class and economic fundament—an ideological maneuver that allows them to support whites against blacks in hopes of mobilizing the working-class racist vote for an economic "populist." Many liberals will plead "color blindness" at election time in order to preserve the myth of democratic equality. Most people, of course, simply shut race out of their mind when not actively expressing contempt or practicing violence against the nearest minority target. But because racism is a paradigm for every other ideology of exclusion, campaigns to combat it—black political campaigns—can provide an example for every other struggle in the system.

Jackson's "rainbow coalition" is an attempt to organize the political strength of all deprived and rejected constituencies around the moral force and political energy of the black movement. It is no gimmick, and although Jackson may throw the term around too breezily, he is deadly serious about it. It is the essence of his campaign.

"The civil rights movement . . . laid the foundations, provided the climate and in many instances trained the initial organizers of the women's, gay, anti-nuclear, environmental and other movements of the seventies and eighties," he told the audience at the gay Human Rights Campaign Fund dinner in New York. "Discrimination, oppression and on occasion genocide have been used to force blacks, women and Native Americans into their proper place. All of us feel deprived in twentieth-century America, and America is still organized by cash—the cash system that is still dominated by white males."

The political demands of the rainbow coalition, implicit in its construction and explicit in Jackson's speeches, are extraordinary. They are racial, sexual, economic and ideological. What other major-party candidate in this century has talked about deprivation in a "cash system dominated by white males"? No wonder Jackson is scaring conventional politicians half to death.

Bruce Bolling, Boston's black city councilor, told a reporter last spring that Jackson "may be viewed as threatening. He's talking about a coalition of people on the outside, and in some quarters people might be anxious about that kind of direction."

It is enormously difficult to convince even a fraction of the "people on the outside" that their interests lie in political coalition, and even harder to talk them all into accepting black leadership—much less Jesse Jackson. And yet it makes perfect sense. The Democrats understand it, but their coalitions have always served the purposes of the white male cash system. Jackson's campaign would establish an opposition to that dominance.

For its part, the Democratic Party leadership seems to have given up on opposition. It has supported Reagan in his imperial invasions; it has grown silent in the face of the business recovery; it has adopted "neoliberal" prejudices against labor, the poor, social welfare and economic redistribution. It is left to Jesse Jackson to stake out opposition ground on America's intervention in Lebanon and the invasion of Grenada, for instance; on the nuclear arms race and corporate accountability and racial equity. It would hardly be an election campaign without him.

It should be said, although it hardly needs saying, that the contradictions in his candidacy and in the black political movement are heavy enough to bring the whole thing down at any time with just a little shoving. There will be plenty of that. Jackson's personality, background, faults and foibles will be excruciatingly exploited. He is so far out of the mold of the typical political candidate that almost everything he ever said or did, or says or does, can be used to invalidate his effort. Is the bookkeeping at PUSH (his Chicago-based organization, People United to Serve Humanity) messy? Did he say the wrong thing on abortion? Did he offend Jews, social democrats, environmentalists, lesbians? Probably. He makes a lot of mistakes, even in his own terms. But until now, at least, he had not been crafting a serious bid for the presidency, and he has not stopped along the way to think that everything can, and will, be used against him.

~ 1989 ~
Beat the Devil
Alexander Cockburn

In his biweekly "Beat the Devil" column on the press and
politics, Alexander Cockburn frequently debunks popular
theories on poverty and race. His newest collection of essays
is *The Golden Age Is In Us: Journeys & Encounters* (Verso).

July 24/31, 1989 ~ There's probably no newspaper in the corporate mainstream that has not, at one time or another, whacked the black poor on the
head with the bludgeon of Senator Pat Moynihan's views: the black family's
"tangle of pathology," the "internal" nature of the black poor's problems,
hence the need for self-help by the black poor and for merciless tough-
mindedness on the part of whites.

The notion that poor people bring their suffering upon themselves is
certainly a lot older than Senator Moynihan, but it's hard to think of
another North American over the past quarter-century who has given the
rich and their agents so much assistance in the task of keeping it
respectably at the forefront of their minds. Anyone wanting to review the
promotion and durability of the Moynihan thesis at the all-important level
of editorial page, news column and TV discussion can now turn to Carl
Ginsburg's excellent *Race and Media*. What follows is drawn entirely from
his monograph.

Moynihan was at the Labor Department when he and his team drafted
"The Negro Family: The Case for National Action" and injected it into the
nation's bloodstream in 1965, at precisely the moment the propertied class
needed to be let off the hook. Think about poverty, the report said, and you
have to think about the black family. No meaningful change is possible
until that family is strengthened "from within." In other words, Pauper,
heal thyself!

Moynihan's thesis first crept into executive discourse on June 4, 1965,
when President Johnson spoke at Howard University. "Negro poverty is
not white poverty," Johnson told his audience. "There are differences . . .
radiating painful roots into the community and into the family and nature
of the individual." Moynihan had apparently sent his report to Johnson's

assistant Bill Moyers, who urged it as the basis for Johnson's speech. This, as we shall see, was not the last time Moyers pressed Moynihan's thoughts upon the public. Tom Wicker's story next day on the front page of *The New York Times* praised the speech hotly, as did a *Times* editorial on June 6 and as did Mary McGrory in *The Washington Star*. *The Washington Post* said with ominous vagueness, "Implicit in his discussion is the fact that the government cannot reach all these sources of maladjustment, except in a remote way."

Notice the extraordinary rapidity with which these "liberals," prompted by Johnson's aides, grasped the point. In the months that followed, the chorus swelled. "Promoting self-help," *The Wall Street Journal* announced in late July, "must realistically appear as a large part of the ultimate answer." In early August, *Newsweek* was invoking Moynihan's famous phrase "tangle of pathology" apropos the black family and saying of the "Negro family problem" that "its very intimacy has excluded it from the public dialogue on civil rights; it reaches too deep into white prejudices and Negro sensitivities." (Translation: all that racist talk about shiftless blacks is true; pass the word along.)

Sliding, with time, into Nixon's camp, Moynihan sharpened his message, urging that black have-nots be treated with "benign neglect" and honoring the haves as he did so in a memo to Nixon "leaked" to the press in the spring of 1970: "We have almost deliberately obscured the extraordinary progress, and commitment to progress, which the nation as a whole has made, which white America has not abandoned, and which increasingly black America is learning to make use of." From here the leap was not far to the theory that integration had achieved "irreversible" momentum, and therefore did not need any further encouragement from the nation's government or courts.

Having thus taught the ruling orders to blame the victim, Moynihan was propelled into his Senate seat in 1976 by *The New York Times*, nicely ensconced against the day of the Second Coming of his report in the Reagan years, when its comforting properties were once more in urgent demand.

Amid the ravages of the 1982-83 recession in Reagan's first term it did not escape the attention of news editors that there were a lot of needy and desperate people about. By 1982 black unemployment approached 20 percent. The reasons for this were as obvious as the misery such numbers implied. Reagan's agenda, scarcely secret, was to lower the costs of production and redistribute wealth upward.

At the end of 1983 the *Baltimore Evening Sun* studied black families for three months and confided to its readers that "state and local officials describe the breakdown in black family structure as one of the biggest and most perplexing problems confronting the city." Nowhere, in any of the articles, was there a mention of economic crisis, corporate policies, management agendas or their effects on the poor. In the fall of 1984, with matchless effrontery, Moynihan descended into the valley and shot the wounded: "At long last," he told NBC News, "a new generation [of blacks] is coming along which says this is our problem and we are going to face it. And good for them."

As the 1980s advanced, so did the economic oppression of the poor, particularly the black poor. By 1987, while Reaganites extolled the breadth of general economic "recovery," black unemployment still stood at 13 percent; in 1965, the year of the report, it was 8.1. One out of every three blacks was poor. The median earnings of full-time black male workers fell 10 percent between 1979 and 1987. In the same period more than half of all new full-time jobs paid poverty wages ($11,610) for families of four. With this acceleration in misery came a corresponding rise in resentment among the haves. George Will observed that "millions of blacks are victims of many irresponsible blacks." Twenty years after Watts, from the towers of a downtown reared by dollars withheld from any urban initiative for the poor, the *Los Angeles Times* ran a glowing feature about the virtues of self-help, replete with quotations from the conservative black economist Glenn Loury, a great favorite of the haves, calling for subminimum wages for teenagers and for enterprise zones, thus, as Ginsburg remarks, aiming to solve a situation caused by exploitation by imposing further exploitation.

The New York Times took up the theme, in a front-page article by Lena Williams on June 15, 1986, headlined "Blacks Debating a Greater Stress on Self-Reliance Instead of Aid." In a nation that has not one black C.E.O. in the top thousand corporations, Williams took the trouble to find a group of unidentified blacks asking themselves "whether racism was the cause of some of the problems confronting poor blacks, whether government aid programs had exacerbated the situation by reducing incentives to work and to keep families intact, and whether blacks themselves had to bear some of the blame." "Noticeably," she said, "Mr. Reagan has not become a focal point in the most recent discussions. Some black social scientists and political observers see that as a good sign." During this period you could read huge articles about the homeless that never once thought it fit to mention that Reagan had cut housing subsidies.

Today more black men are in jail than in college. The number of blacks attending college stands at 26 percent, down from 33 percent in 1976. College-educated black men have an unemployment rate four times greater than their white peers. In this painful hour Moynihan's constructs have been more potent than ever, and in January of 1986 got their most ecstatic reiteration in a CBS documentary by Bill Moyers, Moynihan's salesman to Lyndon Johnson.

Moyers's evocation of the "tangle of pathology," visited in this case on some black people in a poor section of Newark, was received by the haves with wild enthusiasm. The documentary, much of it eliciting from teen-agers' detailed accounts of their sex lives, honed in resolutely on "personal responsibility." *The Boston Globe* called it compelling and quoted from the Moynihan report. In *The New York Times*, John Corry praised it for examin-ing a "culturally unpopular topic." This theme of the courage of Moynihan and his epigones in grasping nettles, speaking the unspeakable, etc. is com-mon to many articles, despite the obvious fact that the themes of the report were very popular with the dispensing classes, and that a courageous approach would have been to say that the condition of the poor and of many black Americans in particular was due to capitalism and the political agenda of the overclass. ("Underclass," an essentialist category, like under-world, became very popular in the Reagan years. "Overclass" somehow never caught on.)

By 1988, Pete Hamill was writing in *Esquire* that "there is very little now that whites can do in a direct way for the maimed and hurting citizens of the Underclass." In February of 1989, Morton Kondracke wrote in *The New Republic* that "the crisis of the underclass is so great that probably nothing short of a spiritual renewal in black America would really solve the problem." (Calls by Jesse Jackson for such a spiritual and political renewal had earlier excited Kondracke to torrents of abuse.) In *The Washington Post* in April, Richard Cohen called for a "war" in the inner city and denounced the "pathetic lassitude" of "the underclass" which militates against "the dignity of honest work, the chance to move up the ladder." Why the appeals to war, now symbolized in South Central Los Angeles by police battering rams? What's dignified about cleaning toilets in downtown hotels? Where's the ladder and the robust black middle class?—largely a myth fostered by government to delude white journalists that all blacks can make it if they only try, along the lines of *Stand and Deliver*, reassurance against the reality of class as destiny. In fact, as Ginsburg points out, "blacks have been more 'self-reliant,' by any measure of social adaptability, having survived *despite* government *and* corporate policies aimed at perpet-uating their impoverishment."

After the rape of a white woman in Central Park by black and Latino youths, Edwin Yoder wrote in *The Washington Post* that their actions could not be explained by "environmental factors." Yoder preferred "the theolog-ical alternative to sociological or economic determinism." Thus do we come to Original Sin and Noah's drunken curse on the children of Ham. Maybe in his hours of community service among the poor, Oliver North can further expound the resonances of Holy Writ to such black families as have survived the Moynihan-fueled onslaughts of his former employer.

~ 1994 ~

Does *Brown* Still Matter?

Micaela di Leonardo
[a response]

The Nation's special issue commemorating the fortieth anniversary of the *Brown v. Topeka Board of Education* case included a symposium on how the Supreme Court's 1954 reasoning applied in 1994. Northwestern University professor of anthropology Micaela di Leonardo contributed the following assessment.

May 23, 1994 ~ As Jonathan Kozol documents in *Savage Inequalities*, American public education today is, on the whole, as separate and unequal as it was before the *Brown* decision. And this is due in part to the liberal, class-denying framing of law itself. Anatole France in 1894 commented that "the law, in its majestic equality, forbids the rich as well as the poor to sleep under bridges." His commentary has haunting, tragic application to the American scene one century later.

The Supreme Court's logic in the *Brown* case is in tune with larger currents in American political discourse in this century—looking for right in all the wrong legal and cultural places. The psychologizing emphasis on damage to black children's self-esteem, the poignant exercises with black and white dolls, were and are no doubt valid, but are hardly the most salient factors to adduce in an argument for school integration. There is an eerie parallel with the later *Roe v. Wade* decision. In each case, the Court plumped for an argument—"feeling of inferiority," "right to privacy"—that, in its effacement of the lesser political and economic power afforded to blacks and women, allowed subsequent legislation and policy that clearly contradicted the Court's intent. Rather than following the Court's psychologism and continuing to worry about children's "self-esteem" or the "culture of nihilism" in inner cities, we would do better to fight hard for the democratic principle of radically equalizing all public school funding. Children's feelings and culture, in an egalitarian, well-funded environment, will take care of themselves.

~ 1994 ~

Affirmative Reaction:
The Freedom of Employment Act

Derrick Bell

Forty years after the *Brown v. Topeka Board of Education* case,
The Nation published a special issue on the legacy of the inte-
gration movement and the current state of race relations.
Derrick Bell, a Scholar in Residence at the New York
University School of Law, contributed the following essay.

May 23, 1994 ~ For the past two years I have been suggesting that racism
is a permanent condition in America. I have argued that American racism
is not, as Gunnar Myrdal concluded in his massive study *An American
Dilemma*, an anomaly on our democratic landscape, a holdover from slavery that the nation both wants to cure and is capable of curing. Rather, I
agree with Jennifer Hochschild's *The New American Dilemma* that racism is
a critically important stabilizing factor that enables whites to bond across a
wide socio-economic chasm. Without the deflecting power of racism,
masses of whites would likely wake up and revolt against the severe disad-
vantage they suffer in income and opportunity when compared with those
whites at the top of our system.

Making the "racism is permanent" case has proved relatively easy for
black people who have heard it. Whites are more resistant, running the
gamut from those who are deeply troubled by my thesis but unable to
refute it, to those who angrily reject the idea, charging that I am racist for
even suggesting it. Even so, there is a long leap from concluding that racism
is permanent to predictions that it will generate policies subjecting millions
of people of color to what amounts to forced labor.

This society has always been willing to advance black interests when
those interests coincide with the perceived needs of whites. Indeed, it is
not too much to suggest that all positive racial policies come about in this
way. For example, Lincoln, while personally finding slavery abhorrent,
issued the Emancipation Proclamation only when he recognized that ending slavery would help preserve the Union; the post–Civil War amendments clearly served the political power-preserving interest of Republicans

who had been victorious on the military front but wanted to insure that battles won in the field were not lost on the political scene by too quickly allowing the defeated Southern Democrats back into the halls of Congress. Even the Supreme Court's decision in *Brown v. Topeka Board of Education* illustrates the point. While depriving whites of the status and resource priorities of segregation, *Brown* provided whites in policy-making positions the benefits of economic and political advantages both at home and abroad that followed abandonment of apartheid in our national law. The *Brown* decision, as University of Iowa law professor Mary Dudziak made clear, gave America credibility in the struggle with Communist nations for the hearts and minds of emerging Third World peoples. It offered reassurance to blacks that the precepts of equality and freedom so heralded during World War II might yet be given meaning at home. And, without state-enforced segregation, it opened the way for the South to make the transition from a rural, plantation society to the modern Sunbelt, with all its potential and profit.

On the other hand, serious differences between whites are often resolved through compromises that sacrifice the rights of blacks. The pattern was set in the seventeenth century, when, as Edmund Morgan explains in *American Slavery—American Freedom,* an alliance between poor whites and plantation owners utilized the enslavement of blacks as the bridge across the broad expanse of wealth disparity.

The classic example is the Hayes-Tilden Compromise following the disputed presidential election of 1876. To avoid a threatened new civil war, the nation's political leaders effected a deal that conceded the election to the Republican, Hayes, in return for a commitment to withdraw Northern troops from the South, an action that left the fate of the newly freed blacks to their former masters.

A few decades later, when working-class whites insisted on formal segregation as the price for their continued allegiance to elite policy-makers, they were granted state-supported superior status at the expense of blacks—a support the Supreme Court ratified in 1896 with its "separate but equal" decision in *Plessy v. Ferguson.* Of course, the definitive sacrifice of black rights was made by the Constitution's Framers in 1787 when, to secure the backing of Southern representatives, they approved the Constitution with no fewer than ten provisions directly or indirectly recognizing and protecting property in slaves.

For the reasons stated earlier, after World War II segregation became a luxury the nation could no longer afford. Blatant discrimination fell out of fashion, a fact that some whites in the South learned slowly, much to the embarrassment of the rest of the country. Through the courts, Congress and the media, these Southern whites became the enemy and those peaceful blacks with their white allies became the heroes. It was a sometimes danger-ous but no less glorious time for those of us involved in what we thought would be the final struggle for civil rights.

But while the Jim Crow signs came down after prolonged battles in the courts and on the streets, society quickly devised means to limit the sub-stantive value of the pro–civil rights decisions and the new civil rights laws enacted during the 1960s. The frustrations engendered by these barriers led to the Black Power movement in the middle and late 1960s, a phenomenon that alienated some whites, and the riots in Watts and other places that turned off still more. The real disenchantment came when whites began to recognize that civil rights for blacks meant more than condemning the use of fire hoses and police dogs on peacefully protesting children in a Deep South town. It meant, as well, giving up privileges and priorities long avail-able to whites simply because they were white.

Applying this history to the current social scene can be deeply disturb-ing. Black workers are a disproportionately large percentage of those "downsized" out of jobs, but whites too are victims of the current disem-ployment trend. From 1989 to 1993, the United States lost 1.6 million manufacturing jobs. As the business sections of the papers report almost daily, those losses continue to mount.

With good reason, millions of white Americans are fearful about their jobs, and yet there has been remarkably little criticism of corporate America for its downsizing policies. During the same period, opposition to affirma-tive action programs has increased. Callers and audience participants on a Phil Donahue show strongly indicated their view that anti-black feelings were a predictable reaction to affirmative action policies. Donahue, trying to ease the tension, said, tongue-in-cheek, "Yes, I know. Every white per-son in America has a relative who lost out on a job or promotion to a less-qualified black person." To his chagrin, the audience broke into wild applause. Caught up in the myth they find comforting, they missed Donahue's effort to use humor to illustrate a truth they are determined not to see.

The fact is that we are at the end of an era when work was the society's sustaining force. We can expect serious dislocations that government—influenced as it is by those who are either profiting from or willing to main-tain the economic status quo—will find it difficult to address in any effec-tive fashion. The likely result will be a move to the political right and a growing antipathy toward this society's traditional scapegoats: black people.

~ 1995 ~

Subject to Debate

Katha Pollitt

Katha Pollitt, an award-winning poet, critic and journalist, writes a biweekly column, "Subject to Debate," for *The Nation* on feminism, politics and culture. Her new book, *Reasonable Creatures: Essays on Women and Feminism* (Knopf), collects much of her recent work.

March 13, 1995 ~ When people argue that we don't need affirmative action anymore, I remember an interchange I had a few years ago with the friendly mom who was showing me around her child's preschool. The place was adorable, I agreed, the teachers imaginative and kind, and no question my daughter would be happy there. But where were the children of color? It's a problem, the mother agreed with a rueful smile. We just don't seem to be able to find them! Then she brightened: Next year would be different—one family would be sending its adopted Chinese toddler, another its adopted Paraguayan. The school was so excited!

You may laugh at this peculiar definition of multiculturalism. Did she think the little Paraguayan would show up wearing a serape and tootling a wooden flute? But this was not Mississippi or Cicero, or even, God forbid, Long Island. This was the Upper West Side of Manhattan, the most liberal Congressional district in America and, at least on paper, one of the most racially integrated neighborhoods in New York City, where people still read *The Village Voice* for its politics and the churches can't decide whether to be early-music concert halls or soup kitchens. If the Good Woman of West End Avenue "can't find" black and Hispanic and Asian children to share her child's classroom, and persuades herself that cultural diversity can be handily supplied by foreign adoption, how likely is it that the country as a whole has reached *either* the color-blind society conservatives claim to want, or the delight-in-difference that multiculturalists promote?

Across the media spectrum, opinion journalists have been falling over themselves to depict the 1994 elections as the White Man's Revenge, and affirmative action seems to be emerging as the chief culprit, worse even than the Antioch dating rules or deconstructionism. On talk radio, where Angry White Males conduct their drumming sessions, Al on his car phone and Joe in Chicago speak openly of blacks and Hispanics as unqualified, lazy and stupid. In the mainstream media, the objection is put differently. The civil rights movement has been such a success that affirmative action is unnecessary, say Linda Chavez, George Will and the other usual suspects; to rightward-moving liberals like Jim Sleeper, it's a bureaucractic hindrance that fuels white resentment and condescends to deserving non-whites.

I'm not sure whether those who make these arguments are naïve or devious. But in my little corner of the work world—liberal opinion magazines—nothing could be further from the truth.

In the thirteen years I've been associated with *The Nation*, we've had exactly one nonwhite person (briefly) on our editorial staff of thirteen, despite considerable turnover. And we're not alone: *The Atlantic* has zero nonwhites out of an editorial staff of twenty-one; *Harper's*, zero out of fourteen; *The New York Review of Books*, zero out of nine; *The Utne Reader*, zero out of twelve. A few do a little better, although nothing to cheer about: *The Progressive*, one out of six; *Mother Jones*, one out of seven; *In These Times*, one out of nine; *The New Republic*, two out of twenty-two; *The New Yorker*, either three or six, depending on how you define "editorial," out of 100 plus. Interestingly, in view of the bromide about feminism as a white women's movement to which nonwhite women are justifiably indifferent or hostile, *Ms.* comes off rather well, with three out of eleven, including the editor-in-chief, Marcia Ann Gillespie. (These figures do not include columnists, correspondents or contributing editors, who are overwhelmingly white, and at *The Nation* exclusively so.)

My point is not to bite the hand that feeds me, or to attack particular people. Clearly, if so many liberal magazines share this particular limitation thirty-one years after the passage of the Civil Rights Act (and five years before the opening of the twenty-first century), something more is at issue than personalities. Nor do I wish to dwell on the hypocrisy factor, the liberal genius for avoiding the medicine one prescribes for others, for claiming extenuating circumstances one would never accept for one's political opponents, and for confusing, like that preschool mom, a heart in the right place with a major talent for cognitive dissonance. On second thought, let me dwell—because surely the widely noted and much-ridiculed ineffectuality of liberal politics is connected to the inability of that vision to command even its own adherents. If we don't live our politics, why should anyone else? Maybe the personnel is the political.

The real lesson I draw from these demographics, though, is that far from living in the color-blind America of conservative fantasies, or the multicultural America of left-wing ones, we still live in a society that is segregated in many ways. People are carefully slotted—and slot them-selves—into remarkably precise positions in a complex class, racial and social order that then determines what they see and what they know. For that preschool mom, reality was families exactly like her own. For the denizens of the tiny cocktail party that is liberal journalism, it's the other denizens, plus their friends, classmates and former students and interns, plus all those people's grown children and *their* friends, all twined togeth-er in an eternal golden braid of networking and schmooze. The workplace is white because the social world is white, and vice versa. Merit doesn't really come into it.

It was to break open such closed worlds that affirmative action was originally designed. And, it's important to note, the benefits are not one-sided. Affirmative action would not only diversify our offices, it would invigorate our pages, which sure could use new voices, new perspectives, new questions. It might even—who knows?—refresh our politics.

Racial integration. It's such a crazy idea, it just might work.

Chapter Three

~

PROFILES OF HOPE & RAGE

Mrs. Fannie Lou Hamer

June 1, 1964 by R. Earl

~ 1958 ~

W.E.B. Du Bois:
Prophet in Limbo

Truman Nelson

Writer and historian Truman Nelson was the author of numerous historical novels on slavery, racism and radical leaders, including *The Sin of the Prophet* (1952) and *The Old Man: John Brown at Harper's Ferry* (1973).

~

This is the modern paradox of Sin before which the Puritan stands open-mouthed and mute. A group, a nation, or a race commits murder and rape, steals and destroys, yet no individual is guilty, no one is to blame, no one can be punished. The black world squirms beneath the feet of the white in impotent fury or sullen hate.

—W. E. B. Du Bois

JANUARY 25, 1958 ~ Here is the unmistakable wrath of a prophet; said yesterday, true today. We listened for it in the deep shame of our recent past to lift us above the brute realities of an American governor punishing the innocent and rewarding a guilty and bestial mob, putting armed troops in the service of its capricious inhumanity. Politicians have since resolved the crisis with counterforce; yet somehow along the way all principle was drained out of the solution.

We scarcely know where to look for the prophets. They are well-nigh obsolete. Being one thing to all men today is a superhuman task, for amplitude is the deadly foe of consistency. We don't sit under preaching any more. No longer can mystic fervor and exhortation make up for error, nor can the proclamation of an absolute make people see things not as they are, but in the shape of old prophecies. There are no more absolutes and yet the prophet has to move from certainty to certainty, break through to reality and then, on center, proclaim it to the world.

Dr. William E. Burghardt Du Bois prepared for his calling as a child of his age, which is of this age, of course, although his life span has been so great that it is only because the prophet has eternal life that we know that he is of our age and younger than we are because he is also of the next age and the next. He was born three years after the War of the Rebellion and under the Presidency of a man unusually sensitive toward white rights masquerading as State's Rights—Andrew Johnson. Time whirled him downstream to his abiding rock with perfunctory ease. He was of mixed blood in a country town in Western Massachusetts where the color line was manifest but not absolutely drawn. To the world he was a Negro, but he did not feel the sting of this at first because he was also poor and this was enough. Somehow, by the staggering economic travail of his mother, he managed to get a first-rate education. However, there are so many elements of the prodigious in this process that it is hard to rate it simply as an achievement; there are too many intangibles—fate, luck, what you will—to dwell on the Horatio Algerish rise of a poor Negro boy in a small town to the eminence of a graduate of Fisk, Harvard and the University of Berlin. He says himself: "It was difficult for me at this time to form a critical estimate of any meaning of the world which differed from the conventional unanimity about me."

So far he had proved nothing but that he was a prodigy. For all this had little to do with his real work, although he thought it had. He thought knowledge was power. It goes without saying (but it should be said at every opportunity) that every Negro in America knows as soon as he is out of his diapers that he is the *Accursed Question;* the Problem settles massively on his young shoulders for life at the (let us say charitably) tenth personal encounter with a member of the white race. Du Bois, like a young horse feeling his strength and destiny as a beast of burden, threw his whole weight into the traces with the thought that if he could just drag the wrongs of his people in a compact load down Main Street something would be done by the passersby. He was at Harvard at one of her greatest periods. He fell under the influence of William James and got from him what he thought would be his ultimate direction: to put science into sociology through a study of his own race. In the slums of Philadelphia, he made monumental studies of Negro morality, urbanization, efforts for social betterment; of the Negro in business, in college, in grade school, in church, at work, in crime: 2,172 pages of scholarly fact and opinion. It made him famous. Platforms were opened to him. Congressional committees sought his testimony . . . voluntary and friendly, of course.

But for all the accuracy and devotion of this truth-seeking, it had slight effect on the daily reality of Negroes being lynched, murdered and starved. The truths were needed but they were not wanted; and the compiler found it easy to starve alongside the subjects of his case histories, suffering the spiritual hunger which is the frustration of the appetite for justice, as well as the physical variety. He then found an enclave of sustenance at Atlanta University, a Negro school, as a teacher.

A functioning prophet has to get hold of some great and crescive phrase, a thought that can ring out in sorrow and in anger and which can be reiterated all his life: in battle from the housetops, in ecstasy among his brethren, in solitude and despair with a succoring and replenishing life. Alas, what a fine thing it would be if thesis-writing could change the world! Our graduate schools would become the Parliament of Man.

What Du Bois got hold of was this: *Most men in this world are colored. A faith in humanity, therefore, a belief in the gradual growth and perfectibility of men must, if honest, be primarily a belief in colored men.*

Anyone can see the enormous power of these thirty-two words over the 2,172 pages of thesis-writing. The credo begins with a rude shock to the dominant whites; it challenges their ethics, strips naked their hypocrisy, universalizes their religions and then puts them on their good behavior, tested by their own great shibboleth of "democracy." Every gift, every bravery, every defeat in Du Bois flowered out of this. It brought him into his first great struggle.

Du Bois did this and more: he attacked the great hero of his own people. It takes a brave Catholic to take issue with the Pope, a brave Jew to denounce or disown Moses: Booker T. Washington was both of these for ten million Negroes at the turn of the century. Du Bois and Washington had a host of differences but the salient one was that Washington believed that the Negro's struggle out of the prison of his skin must be subordinated to dominant public opinion and that opinion deferred to and cajoled until it allowed a deviation toward better ways (he seems to be haunting the Executive Mansion today). During Washington's period as spokesman for the race, the whole body of Jim Crow caste laws was passed in the South, there were hundreds of lynchings yearly and murderous incidents and degradations; but the ringleader's ideological emphasis was on *Negro* shortcomings, so that the onus was placed on the Negro himself. Andrew Carnegie made Washington a gift of $600,000 for Tuskegee; other rich whites were generous.

Du Bois, almost single-handed, shattered these golden chains. He crossed the water into Canada, like John Brown before him, to mobilize a program of revolt against voluntary segregation. The Niagara Movement is a book in itself; it cannot be summarized other than by saying it demanded *practical* equality as John Brown demanded *practical* abolition—the full and unequivocal equality of the Negro in all areas of the human condition. Now! At once! Why not?

Du Bois was nearly inundated by sewer-pipe torrents of criticism from all sides, but he worked on in semi-secrecy to develop the mobilization and the next year, in one of the most moving organizational incidents in human history, the black men of the Niagara Movement met at Harper's Ferry and walked barefoot over the flinty roads in a pilgrimage to the site of the Engine House. They stood there, in the broad and southern daylight and with their bare flesh pressing on the spot marked by the sacrificial blood of the white man who had most plainly burned the poison of white supremacy out of himself and his children, dedicated themselves to a program of positive, non-violent action based on these truths addressed to the American Conscience:

> We want manhood suffrage and we want it now, henceforth and forever. We want the Constitution of the country enforced: Congress to take charge of Congressional elections, the Fourteenth Amendment to be carried out to the letter and every state disenfranchised in Congress which attempts to disenfranchise its rightful voters. We want black boys and girls to know, to think, to aspire. We will get these things by voting where we can vote, by persisting, unceasing agitation, by hammering at the truth, by sacrifice and work. We do not believe in violence but we do believe in John Brown, in that incarnate spirit of justice . . . and here on the scene of John Brown's martyrdom, we reconsecrate ourselves, our honor, our property, to the final emancipation of the race which John Brown died to make free.

This was Du Bois in 1906. The date is crucial, for it was a time when Southern white attitudes were not as basaltic as they are now; it was the very date on which Alabama led the South by instituting the first legal Jim Crow car (C. Vann Woodward, in his immensely valuable research, has completely destroyed the sanctimonious myth of the antiquity of segregation). There was still time before the deluge, Du Bois thought, to solve the American dilemma by implementing the amendments in the Constitution which guaranteed political equality to the Negro. In terms of the foot-dragging going on today, it may seem madness to have called for equality fifty years ago, but competent sociologists such as Kenneth B. Clark of New York City College are saying that the whole concept of "gradualism" in race issues is generally seen by its opponents as a sign of weakness, and, furthermore, grants them time to mobilize, organize and intensify their opposition. It was *after* Du Bois' call for full suffrage and rights, specifically when the election of Woodrow Wilson in 1912 brought the Southern Democrats back to Washington in force for the first time since the War of the Rebellion, that the great tide of segregation swept to its high-water mark.

There is considerable evidence today that a speedy and forthright approach to racial problems is less likely than gradualism to result in bitter and prolonged opposition. It is not hard to believe that it might have been possible for Negroes, had they listened to true and not false prophets fifty years past, to have had their full rights long ago.

The big flaw in this crystal is that there was no N.A.A.C.P. then, but there wouldn't have been any N.A.A.C.P. today either, if it had not been for Du Bois. None of the people in this great organization want contention over claims to foundership. Some say Oswald Garrison Villard started it. He was, perhaps, its first real functionary. Some say William Walling. The Association itself says Walling, Mary White Ovington and Henry Moskowitz laid the foundations, but anyone who has grieved at the plunging gulf separating the communication of black and white in this country today knows instinctively that no three whites, no matter how enlightened, could ever appear other than (in the words of the old Wobbly song) "condescending saviors" to the Negro people, unless and until some of their own folks entered the Association on equal terms.

It was Du Bois who fertilized this seedling and made it viable by leading into it the brave black men of his Niagara Movement. Oswald Garrison Villard, to his eternal credit, saw the *man* in Du Bois and let him establish and operate *The Crisis*, one of the great agitational organs of world reform. It was great because it was not the stultified and broad-beamed expression of committee decisions, but struck out with the hard, sword-shaped convictions of one man. The Association recognized its greatness when Du Bois left this post, saying:

> He founded *The Crisis* without a cent of capital and made it self-supporting, with a peak circulation of 100,000. He transformed the Negro world, created what had never existed before, a Negro intelligentsia. He gave a new orientation to the relationship of the black and white races. Without him the Association would never have been what it was and is.

From the towering and broad-margined plateau of his prophecy, Du Bois could see Africa, the Negro homeland, where the black man really was the majority. At the close of World War I, a disaster he blamed on

European rivalries over the exploitation of colored, colonial labor, he went to Versailles to take Wilson up on his pledge of self-determination to small nations. What about the small nations of Africa? he asked, and organized the first *genuine* Pan-African Congress. From then on he was the acknowledged "Father of Pan-Africanism," founding and keeping alive the African Renaissance, seeking liberation from colonialism.

Du Bois has been rewarded as this country nearly always rewards its prophets. He was arrested—as Thoreau was arrested, and Theodore Parker and Garrison, Phillips, Samuel Gridley Howe, Bronson Alcott, Abner Kneeland, Frank Sanborn, T. W. Higginson, Ezra Heywood, Benjamin Tucker, Sacco and Vanzetti. The charge made against Du Bois was that he was an agent of a foreign power. He was acquitted. But the same man who had been equated with Franklin and Jefferson by Henry Steele Commager in his *Men Who Make Up Our Minds*, described by John Gunther as "almost like Shaw or Einstein . . . in his field," who was given the most eloquent praise by Van Wyck Brooks, Eugene O'Neill and others of like caliber, discovered after he had been fingerprinted, handcuffed, bailed and remanded for trial, that a terrible blight seemed to settle over his virtues and his powers. He found himself virtually excluded from the press and publishing; found that he was in exile, shut off from the main channel of American life which he had generously purified and deepened in his long lifetime. Not only exiled, but entombed: he could not get a passport to go abroad and express himself.

It must be said that Du Bois has been arrogant and made some critical misjudgments. Don't ask me when. I am an intemperate man myself. My explanation is that we ordinary men who bruise easily and do not suffer fools gladly, and *all* prophets, are constitutionally wrong-headed and arrogant. Garrison and Phillips drove with the whiplash of their vituperation every middle-of-the-roader out of their faction of the anti-slavery movement. Theodore Parker was the most hated man of his time among his brethren of the cloth. Perhaps this is the best thing about them, and the element which might have saved the radical movement in this country from its present chaos and futility: the ability to make something monolithic about dissent, instead of the other way around where a thing is said to be monolithic because there is no apparent or permitted dissent and it suddenly falls to pieces like rotten cheese. Du Bois was just wrong-headed enough fifty years ago to reverse the direction of a race and demand full equality as a minimum when most Negroes were learning how to be quiet enough not to be lynched.

His own excuse is less flattering. He says:

My leadership was a leadership solely of ideas. I never was, nor ever will be, personally popular. This was not simply because of my idiosyncrasies, but because I despise the essential demagoguery of personal leadership; of that hypnotic ascendancy over men which carries out objectives regardless of their value or validity simply by personal loyalty and admiration. In my case I withdrew sometimes ostentatiously from the personal nexus, but I sought all the more repeatedly to force home essential ideas.

He is arrogant enough today, after suffering this blight six years ago, in his eighty-third year, not to crawl, to breast-beat, to cry *mea culpa*, and so get himself fumigated, deodorized and acceptable, but rather to sit in solitude, waiting for the American people to rehabilitate themselves in relation to *him* instead of the other way around. This is the way it has to be with prophets. He is in solitude, but not in silence. He is working, and let this be an example to the fearful men of this cardiac age to whom death lurks conspiratorially in the shadow of every peak of tension, emotion or commonplace effort. He has just written a trilogy on Negro history to complete his life's message. The first volume appeared in 1957; the others are to appear this year and next. He is nearly ninety and has endured every variety of abuse, accusation and infamy, and all this with a nature sensitive to an extraordinary degree; endured it for his color, his religion, his politics and most of all for the sheer, cussed unchangeability of his *self*.

Take a long look at this man. Historians and textbook writers have a way of making his kind invisible and hanging their laurels on political accidents. I know just how they do it. There is evil and a man challenges it and in the ensuing struggle people find themselves involved, willy-nilly, on his side. And they suffer for it and blame him for calling attention to the evil and in a generation or so he has been transformed into the evil itself.

But this does not have to be. Someday the people in this country will demand that their own records be set straight, and alongside the political accidents, the Presidents and Senators, will go the enduring and usable truths of the American Prophets. Among these Prophets will be W. E. B. Du Bois.

~ 1964 ~

Tired of Being Sick and Tired

Jerry DeMuth

In 1964, the journalist Jerry DeMuth visited and talked to Fannie Lou Hamer, who had just co-founded the Mississippi Freedom Democratic Party.

JUNE 1, 1964 ~ About 20 feet back from a narrow dirt road just off the state highway that cuts through Ruleville, Miss., is a small, three-room, white frame house with a screened porch. A large pecan tree grows in the front yard and two smaller ones grow out back. Butter bean and okra plants are filling out in the gardens on the lots on either side of the house. Lafayette Street is as quiet as the rest of Ruleville, a town of less than 2,000 located in Sunflower County, 30 miles from the Mississippi River. Sunflower County, home of Senator Eastland and 68 percent Negro, is one of twenty-four counties in the northwestern quarter of the state—the Delta—that make up the Second Congressional District. Since 1941, this district has been represented in Congress by Jamie Whitten, chairman of the House Appropriations Subcommittee on Agriculture, who is now seeking his thirteenth term.

From the house on the dirt road there now comes a person to challenge Jamie Whitten: Mrs. Fannie Lou Hamer. Mrs. Hamer is a Negro and only 6,616 Negroes (or 4.14 percent of voting-age Negroes) were registered to vote in the Second Congressional District in 1960. In 1962, when Whitten was elected for the twelfth time, only 31,345 persons cast votes, although there were more than 300,000 persons of voting age in the district, 59 percent of them Negro.

Until Mississippi stops its discriminatory voting practices, Mrs. Hamer's chance of election is slight, but she is waking up the citizens of her district. "I'm showing people that a Negro can run for office," she explains. Her deep, powerful voice shakes the air as she sits on the porch or inside, talking to friends, relatives and neighbors who drop by on the one day each week when she is not out campaigning. Whatever she is talking about soon becomes an impassioned plea for a change in the system that exploits the Delta Negroes. "All my life I've been sick and tired," she shakes her head.

"Now I'm sick and tired of being sick and tired."

Mrs. Hamer was born October 6, 1917, in Montgomery County, the twentieth child in a family of six girls and fourteen boys. When she was 2 her family moved to Sunflower County, 60 miles to the west.

> The family would pick fifty-sixty bales of cotton a year, so my father decided to rent some land. He bought some mules and a cultivator. We were doin' pretty well. He even started to fix up the house real nice and had bought a car. Then our stock got poisoned. We knowed this white man had done it. He stirred up a gallon of Paris green with the feed. When we got out there, one mule was already dead. T'other two mules and the cow had their stomachs all swelled up. It was too late to save 'em. That poisonin' knocked us right back down flat. We never did get back up again. That white man did it just because we were gettin' somewhere. White people never like to see Negroes get a little success. All of this stuff is no secret in the state of Mississippi.
>
> We went back to sharecroppin', halvin', it's called. You split the cotton half and half with the plantation owner. But the seed, fertilizer, cost of hired hands, everything is paid out of the cropper's half.
>
> Later, I dropped out of school. I cut corn stalks to help the family. My parents were gettin' up in age—they weren't young when I was born, I was the twentieth child—and my mother had a bad eye. She was cleanin' up the owner's yard for a quarter when somethin' flew up and hit her in the eye.
>
> So many times for dinner we would have greens with no seasonin' . . . and flour gravy. My mother would mix flour with a little grease and try to make gravy out of it. Sometimes she'd cook a little meal and we'd have bread.
>
> No one can honestly say Negroes are satisfied. We've only been patient, but how much more patience can we have?

Fannie Lou and Perry Hamer have two daughters, 10 and 19, both of whom they adopted. The older girl left school after the tenth grade to begin working. Several months ago when she tried to get a job, the employer commented, "You certainly talk like Fannie Lou." When the girl replied, "She raised me," she was denied the job. She has a job now, but Mrs. Hamer explains, "They don't know she's my child."

The intimidation that Mrs. Hamer's older girl faces is what Mrs. Hamer has faced since August 31, 1962. On that day she and seventeen others went down to the county courthouse in Indianola to try to register to vote. From the moment they arrived, police wandered around their bus, keeping an eye on the eighteen. "I wonder what they'll do," the bus driver said to Mrs. Hamer. Halfway back to Ruleville, the police stopped the bus and ordered it back to Indianola. There they were all arrested. The bus was painted the wrong color, the police told them.

She didn't pass the test the first time, so she returned on December 4, and took it again. "You'll see me every 30 days till I pass," she told the registrar. On January 10, she returned and found out that she had passed. "But I still wasn't allowed to vote last fall because I didn't have two poll-tax receipts. We still have to pay poll tax for state elections. I have two receipts now."

After being forced to leave the plantation, Mrs. Hamer stayed with various friends and relatives. On September 10, night riders fired sixteen times into the house of one of these persons, Mrs. Turner. Mrs. Hamer was away at the time. In December, 1962, the Hamers moved into their present home which they rent from a Negro woman.

Mrs. Hamer had by then begun active work in the civil rights movement. She gathered names for a petition to obtain federal commodities for needy Negro families and attended various Southern Christian Leadership Conference (SCLC) and Student Nonviolent Coordinating Committee (SNCC) workshops throughout the South. Since then she has been active as a SNCC field secretary in voter registration and welfare programs and has taught classes for SCLC. At present, most of her time is spent campaigning.

In June of last year, Mrs. Hamer was returning from a workshop in Charleston, S.C. She was arrested in Winona, in Montgomery County, 60 miles east of Indianola, the county in which she was born. Along with others, she was taken from the bus to the jail.

They carried me into a room and there was two Negro boys in this room. The state highway patrolman gave them a long, white blackjack and he told one of the boys, "Take this," and the Negro, he said, "This what you want me to use?" The state patrolman said, "That's right, and if you don't use it on her you know what I'll use on you."

I had to get over on a bed flat on my stomach and that man beat me . . . that man beat me till he give out. And by me screamin', it made a plain-clothes man—he didn't have on nuthin' like a uniform—he got so hot and worked up he just run there and started hittin' me on the back of my head. And I was tryin' to guard some of the licks with my hands and they just beat my hands till they turned blue. This Negro just beat me till I know he was give out. Then this state patrolman told the other Negro to take me so he take over from there and he just keep beatin' me.

The police carried Mrs. Hamer to her cell when they were through beating her. They also beat Annelle Ponder, an SCLC worker who was returning on the bus with her, and Lawrence Guyot, a SNCC field secretary who had traveled from the Greenwood SNCC office to investigate the arrests.

They whipped Annelle Ponder and I heard her screamin'. After a while she passed by where I was in the cell and her mouth was bleedin' and her hair was standin' up on her head and you know it was horrifyin'.
Over in the night I even heard screamin'. I said, "Oh, Lord, somebody else gettin' it, too." It was later that we heard that Lawrence Guyot was there, I got to see him. I could walk as far as the cell door and I asked to please leave that door open so I could get a breath of fresh air every once in a while. That's how I got to see Guyot. He looked as if he was in pretty bad shape. And it was on my nerves, too, because that was the first time I had seen him and not smilin'.
After I got out of jail, half dead, I found out that Medgar Evers had been shot down in his own yard.
We're tired of all this beatin', we're tired of takin' this. It's been a hundred years and we're still being beaten and shot at, crosses are still being burned, because we want to vote. But I'm goin' to stay in Mississippi and if they shoot me down, I'll be buried here.

Obviously, Fannie Lou Hamer will not be easily stopped. "We mean to use every means to try and win. If I lose we have this freedom registration and freedom vote to see how many would have voted if there wasn't all this red tape and discrimination." If Mrs. Hamer is defeated by Jamie Whitten in the primary, she will also file as an independent in the general election.
A Mississippi Freedom Democratic Party is also being formed which will hold meetings on every level within the state, from precinct on up, finally choosing a delegation to the National Democratic Convention that will challenge the seating of the regular all-white Mississippi delegation.
In addition to Mrs. Hamer, three other Mississippi Negroes are running for national office in the 1964 elections.
This extensive program provides a basis for Negroes organizing throughout the state, and gives a strong democratic base for the Freedom Democratic Party. The wide range of Negro participation will show that the problem in Mississippi is not Negro apathy, but discrimination and fear of physical and economic reprisals for attempting to register.
The Freedom Democratic candidates will also give Mississippians, white

as well as Negro, a chance to vote for candidates who do not stand for political, social and economic exploitation and discrimination, and a chance to vote for the National Democratic ticket rather than the Mississippi slate of unpledged electors.

"We've been waitin' all our lives," Mrs. Hamer exclaims, "and still gettin' killed, still gettin' hung, still gettin' beat to death. Now we're tired waitin'!"

~ 1969 ~

Life on the Line:
Conversation with Cleaver

Henry E. Weinstein

Henry E. Weinstein, then a freelance writer and law student, interviewed Black Panther leader Eldridge Cleaver in November 1968, just before Cleaver returned to prison for a parole violation.

JANUARY 20, 1969 ~

Weinstein: Many of your public statements and also comments in *Soul on Ice* indicate that you think education and work with young people is extremely important. In this context what is the relationship of the Black Panther Party to black student union groups on high school and college campuses?

Cleaver: We have had good relationships with the black student unions at local high schools; indeed some of them have changed their name to Black Panther student unions.

The situation on the college campuses has been different. Before forming the Black Panther Party, Bobby Seale and Huey Newton tried to do some organizing at Merritt College, where they were students. They started the Soul Students group at Merritt. They discovered that there are problems with starting a revolutionary movement among blacks at the college level because almost all black college students are from the black bourgeoisie.

The black middle class are the most alienated from their roots; when the idea of black consciousness began to develop they had the furthest to go. Curiously enough, though, you also had the development of what is called "cultural nationalism" and some of this was a form of black racism.

Another problem has been the compartmentalization of black college students. They have been viewed as a separate entity, but they must be seen as part of the larger community. They must be united to that larger community so that these groups can function together. This goes for white students as well. They have compartmentalized themselves too. Liberation must come and can only come from the entire community, not just from the colleges.

Weinstein: Huey Newton has been imprisoned; and you are due to go back to jail in a few days. Thus a significant portion of the leadership of the Black Panther Party will have been put out of circulation in one form or other. What have you been doing to develop new leadership?

Cleaver: This is obviously an important problem. We are continuously trying to develop new leadership in the party. We have some people ready to take over if the current leadership is put in jail, or something similar, but not enough. We want the Black Panther Party to be a self-perpetuating group, not a one-man organization.

Weinstein: Many individuals do not seem to understand the meaning of some of your rhetoric. Phrases such as "Free Huey or the Sky's the Limit," for example, have been interpreted in several ways. Could you elaborate upon this?

Cleaver: When we use an expression like "Mickey Mouse Reagan" or "Donald Duck Rafferty," I think it is clear that this is a put-down; it is meant to be derisive. The phrase, "Free Huey or the Sky's the Limit," is also clear, but has broader ramifications. When we say this we mean that Huey must be set free or the country will be destroyed; there should be no misunderstanding about this.

But you also have to consider that when we were saying this before Huey's trial we were engaged in psychological warfare. We were striving for a mass mobilization. We were attempting to educate the public. The establishment uses psychological warfare too. They were trying to railroad Huey Newton into the gas chamber. The Black Panther Party countered by threats and by focusing attention on what was going on in that courthouse. We kept Huey out of the gas chamber, but he still is not free. This is due to the effects that establishment propaganda had on the jury.

"The Sky's the Limit" is an old American term; people should understand it. They just would rather interpret it differently. The police felt that they understood what we meant and that's why 15,000 National Guardsmen were called up, ready to move at the end of the trial. They expected a certain sort of reaction and wanted to wipe out the Black Panther Party. But right after the end of the trial we told all the Panthers to stay off the street that night. Huey said we should carry the legal case as far as possible. This freaked out the cops; two of them shot up our office. This was another form of psychological warfare on our part and it worked to some extent.

This psychological warfare must now move in other directions. But it must be remembered that our actions are always geared to our position and resources. If we could take Huey out of jail forcefully we would, but right now this simply is not possible. So it becomes a question of getting into a position to implement what you have to do. And that is why we still mean it when we say "Free Huey or the Sky's the Limit."

Weinstein: Is your paper staffed solely by blacks, and if so how does this fit in with your coalition with the Peace and Freedom Party?

Cleaver: The paper is put out solely by black people. We do, however, print articles by white people in the paper. I think that this is a policy to be encouraged because the final movement must unite whites and blacks if we are really going to deal with the problems that confront us.

Weinstein: What is the relationship of the Black Panther Party to organizations such as CORE, SNCC and the Mississippi Freedom Labor Union?

Cleaver: We have no relationship to CORE. As far as I am concerned they have become part of the power structure. Their concept of "black capitalism" is merely part of the welfare-capitalist phase of oppression. It is simply another example of indirect control of blacks by the power structure. The forms of exploitation have been modified so as to continue to deceive the oppressed classes.

SNCC was essentially a movement rather than an organization. SNCC never had a membership as such. To do what has to be done in this country you have to include the masses in the machinery of your organization; SNCC couldn't do this. Lately, SNCC has been attempting to make this transition from a movement to an organization.

The movement orientation is certainly a large part of black history in the United States. Such an orientation is now obsolete. There is a pressing need to proceed to the organizational stage.

We need national organizations. We must unite all the regional organizations of blacks, even though they are acting to solve local problems. The Mississippi Freedom Labor Union, which you referred to, is a case in point. At present such a group can have only a transitory effect.

We need a national organization to unite the various efforts into one. That is one of the things the Black Panther Party has been attempting to do. This national organization, however, need not be the Black Panther Party. We would join a better group if such a change becomes necessary. Certain members of SNCC fell into a "reactionary trap" in this regard, and were reluctant to effect certain mergers because of their desire to maintain themselves in positions of power. What we need is merger rather than internecine conflict.

Weinstein: There has been a lot of talk about the potential for a revolutionary movement in this country which would unite blacks, students and poor whites. Yet what seems to be happening is not a revolution on the Left, but a revolution on the Right with lower-middle-class whites rallying behind the standard of George Wallace. Do you see this development as a serious problem?

Cleaver: The people who are supporting Wallace are simple-minded and politically naïve; they do not understand the problems facing this country.

When Wallace renounces the Establishment these people respond to him. But I do not feel they are really sympathetic to his alternatives, so I have no long-range fear of Wallace.

It requires a shrewd mind, however, to understand, deal with, and break through racism in this country. At the present time you have working-class people who are basically comfortable and who won't come into the streets: this is the problem of the Left. Although these people have jobs and are relatively comfortable, they are miserable and dissatisfied. They are suffering spiritually as a result of the oppressive lies that have been imposed upon them. This deterioration of their condition is increasing. Politically conscious people have to make these working-class people see how racism is affecting their lives and project a Left alternative to these problems. That is what it will take to get these "comfortable people" to move.

Weinstein: In recent lectures that you have given at Berkeley and in a current issue of the Black Panther newspaper you have talked at length about the origin and nature of "ethnic power." In terms of this sort of group consciousness, what direction do you see the Black Power movement taking?

Cleaver: We don't want black people to go through the melting pot and perpetuate the system. If this happens, black people will simply be functional lackeys and torpedo the possibility of black liberation. We want to change the system.

The melting-pot theory is the basic myth of the United States. This theory defines the United States strategy and tactics develop from the definitions created by this theory. The melting-pot myth has created an artificial "oneness" that obscures many problems.

The type of ethnocentrism that has developed in the United States is not a good thing if we want the earth to continue to exist. It was once a social apparatus created to survive certain sorts of hostility. It was a protective device. But times have changed, and we need non-ethnocentric people who are able to identify with humanity in a broad sense. This sort of unity is the only way to solve the problems we have here in the United States and in the world.

For example, the Irish, as an oppressed group, used to put pressure on the power structure. But eventually the Irish moved into the system, and their ethnic loyalties soon were manipulated by politicians. The Irish are now among the bourgeoisie, but they are still manipulated by ethnic loyalties. Now these loyalties perpetuate the status quo, and thus many of the Irish are now being manipulated by their enemies. This is indicative of a basic development among ethnic groups in this country—that the ethnics who are in a better position manipulate the less fortunate in their own group.

Weinstein: Revolutions are usually brought about by individuals who feel desperate about their circumstances. As a class students are comfortable, at least in a material sense, as contrasted to blacks. Will coalitions between white students and groups such as the Black Panther Party ultimately break down because of this difference?

Cleaver: Students are not politically naïve in contrast to the white adults we were just talking about. They have a social consciousness. Therefore it doesn't matter if they are well-off materially because their values are affronted by what they see in society. Throughout history we can see revolutions that were led by people who were well-off but had an intellectual and spiritual motivation.

Thus far, students have pursued a course of radical dissent but not that of revolutionary action. It has been like an extended field trip to upset their elders and it has not gone far enough. The students have stopped short of what is needed. They probably won't be willing to take up guns and execute the regents, as they deserve.

The revolutionaries of the future may come from the students when they go out into the world. Some will not be able to find their place in the outside world. But the foundation for a real revolutionary movement is not here yet.

~ 1978 ~

The F.B.I.'s Wildest Dream

Victor Navasky

Victor Navasky, editor of *The Nation* from 1978 to 1994 and currently publisher and editorial director of the magazine, offered readers a firsthand account of the F.B.I.'s revealing views on black leadership, particularly the Rev. Martin Luther King Jr.

JUNE 17, 1978 ~ By now the F.B.I.'s campaign against Martin Luther King has been devastatingly documented.

The Church Committee told us how the bureau used every intelligence-gathering technique at its disposal to obtain information about the "private activities" of Dr. King and his advisers to "completely discredit" them.

We have learned through release of the Freedom of Information Act documents and other revelations how the F.B.I.—responding to the late J. Edgar Hoover's obsession—tried to destroy King's marriage and perhaps attempted to drive him to suicide by threatening to release a tape recording made from microphones hidden in his hotel rooms.

We have read portions of one incredible F.B.I. memorandum after another, including one from the bureau's Domestic Intelligence Division which concluded that his "demagogic speech" at the August 1963 March on Washington established him as the "most dangerous and effective Negro leader in the country."

But perhaps the most menacing memorandum is one that until now has been quoted only in fragments, a memorandum written within days after *Time* named Dr. King as its Man of the Year. On January 8, 1964, Assistant F.B.I. Director William Sullivan sent a memorandum about King to another Hoover assistant, Alan Belmont. As reproduced in the Church Committee report, the memorandum reads as follows:

Subject: Samuel Riley Pierce, Jr.
    We know that Reverend Dr. Martin Luther King *(deletion, deletion)* represents a very real security problem to this country. In addition to *(deletion)*, Dr. King, as we know, for some time now has

been *(deletion)*. Apart from the security factor, he is a disgrace to the Negro people of this country because of his *(deletion)* while at the same time purporting to be a minister of the gospel. Obviously he has the capacity to deceive people very successfully. This was made evident most recently by his being selected by *Time* magazine as the Man of the Year.

Further, we know that he has been able to cleverly deceive both very important Protestant and Catholic organizations, securing thereby support from them which gives him added stature. It should be very clear to all of us that Martin Luther King must, at some propitious point in the future, be revealed to the people of this country and to his Negro followers as being what he actually is—a fraud, demagogue and moral scoundrel. When the true facts concerning his activities are presented, such should be enough, if handled properly, to take him off his pedestal and to reduce him completely in influence so that he will no longer be a security problem and no longer will be deceiving and misleading the Negro people.

When this is done, and it can be and will be done, obviously much confusion will reign, particularly among the Negro people. There will be embarrassment, frustration, confusion, resentment, et cetera. Because of this and the emotional reaction that will set in, it is not unlikely that movements like the Nation of Islam could benefit greatly. Further other ridiculous developments similar to the Old Father Devine and Daddy Grace organizations may appear. The Negroes will be left without a national leader of sufficiently compelling personality to steer them in the proper direction. This is what could happen, but need not happen if the right kind of a national Negro leader could at this time be gradually developed so as to overshadow Dr. King and be in the position to assume the role of the leadership of the Negro people when King has been completely discredited.

For some months I have been thinking about this matter. One day I had an opportunity to explore this from a philosophical and sociological standpoint with *(deletion)* whom I have known for some years. As I previously reported, *(deletion)* is a very able fellow, *(deletion)*, and one on whom I can rely. I asked *(deletion)* to give the matter some attention and if he knew any Negro of outstanding intelligence and ability let me know and we would have a discussion. *(deletion)* has submitted to me the name of the above-captioned person, *(deletion)*.

Enclosed with this memorandum is an outline of *(deletion)* biography which is truly remarkable for a man so young, having been

born (*deletion*), 1932. On scanning this biography, it will be seen
that (*deletion*) does have all the qualifications of the kind of a Negro
I have in mind to advance to positions of national leadership. I
won't go into all his accomplishments and qualifications in this
memorandum, for it will only take a minute or two to scan the
enclosed biography.

On first blush I know it can be said it is not the concern of the
Bureau what happens to the Negroes when Martin Luther King
has been discredited. This can be said, but I think it is a very short-
sighted view. It is our concern if large numbers of them go into the
Nation of Islam and other extremist groups with which we are
concerned as an investigative agency. It is our concern if the
Communist Party would be able to capitalize upon this confusion.
Further, from a positive and constructive standpoint it would be of
great advantage to have leading the Negro people a truly brilliant,
honorable and loyal Negro who would steer the 20 million
Negroes away from communism. I think in a very sound sense this
necessarily must be of great interest to us. It would be most helpful
to have a man like (*deletion*) leading the Negroes to whom we could
go, if necessary, and rely upon in sensitive matters over which this
Bureau has jurisdiction.

I want to make it clear at once that I don't propose that the
F.B.I. in any way become involved openly as the sponsor of a
Negro leader to overshadow Martin Luther King. As far as I am
concerned, this is not an issue at all. But I do propose that I be
given permission to explore further this entire matter with (*deletion*) and any other person known to both (*deletion*) and myself who
could be helpful. If this thing can be set up properly without the
Bureau in any way becoming directly involved, I think it would be
not only a great help to the F.B.I. but would be a fine thing for the
country at large. While I am not specifying at the moment, there
are various ways in which the F.B.I. could give this entire matter
the proper direction and development. There are highly placed
contacts of the F.B.I. who might be very helpful to further such a
step. These can be discussed in detail later when I have probed
more fully into the possibilities.

The memorandum, reproduced on the previous pages, reveals at last the
F.B.I.'s candidate to replace Dr. King and the revelation is, to say the least,
a surprise. The "very able fellow" Sullivan came up with to replace Dr.
King was Samuel R. Pierce Jr.

Judge Pierce had (and presumably still has) impeccable credentials for the world in which he worked. A member of the Park Avenue law firm of Battle, Fowler, Stokes and Kheel, a former General Sessions judge, Assistant District Attorney in New York County and Assistant United States Attorney, a Republican, the only black member of the Army's Criminal Investigation Division, Phi Beta Kappa and a football star at Cornell, he went on to serve in the Nixon administration as General Counsel to the U.S. Treasury Department, to join the executive board of the Boy Scouts of America and to be the first black to sit on two corporate boards of directors, Prudential Life and General Electric.

Had he ever marched in a demonstration, sat in, written a desegregation brief, signed a civil rights petition? What qualities did the blacks want in a leader and why did Dr. King's noble humility inspire and stir a generation? Who knew, and more important, who cared? Certainly not William Sullivan and Alan Belmont and definitely not their superior, J. Edgar Hoover, who scrawled at the bottom of Sullivan's memorandum: "I am glad to see that 'light' has finally, though dismally delayed, come to the Domestic Int. Div. I struggled for months to get over the fact the Communists were taking over the racial movement but our experts here couldn't or wouldn't see it. H."

~ 1984 ~

From Garvey to Jackson

Clayborne Carson

Clayborne Carson is the senior editor of Martin Luther King
Jr.'s papers and a professor of history at Stanford University.

March 31, 1984 ~ Black nationalism is usually seen as a recurrent, extreme
departure from the political mainstream rather than as a continuing mani-
festation of cultural distinctiveness. In part, that mistaken view is a product
of the racial controversies of the 1960s and the adoption during that decade
of black nationalist ideas by militant activists. During the late 1960s and
early 1970s, however, it became apparent that black nationalism was a complex tradition with conservative as well as radical undercurrents.

Misconceptions about black nationalism have been especially evident
in the literature on Marcus Garvey, a gifted orator and organizer whose
meteoric career displayed many facets of the black nationalist tradition.
Arriving in New York City in 1916 with the modest goal of raising money
for an industrial school in his native Jamaica, Garvey was caught up in the
militancy of the years after World War I, when many blacks refused to
endure the widespread racial violence that culminated in the riots of 1919.
Other leaders, such as A. Philip Randolph in *The Messenger* and W.E.B.
Du Bois in *The Crisis*, spoke out against racial injustice, but none attracted
as much organized support. By the early 1920s, Garvey would later boast,
his Universal Negro Improvement Association (U.N.I.A.) had "enrolled
more members throughout the world than almost all other Negro organizations put together."

If the portrait that emerges from the Garvey papers is not that of a black
radical hero, it is also not that of a charlatan without historical importance.
Despite his flamboyant military dress and irascible manner, Garvey was an
astute observer of world affairs and a shrewd analyst of human behavior. He
can best be seen as a transitional figure in the development of black political
thought, for he moved beyond the ideas of earlier nationalists, who were
often elitist in their relations with the masses, and mobilized a large seg-
ment of the black populace. Some aspects of his message seem mundane

and his public pomposity invites ridicule, but Garvey's apparent lack of sophistication contributed to his appeal: he communicated with the black masses in terms they understood rather than in the refined and borrowed vocabulary of the college-educated elite.

The black leaders who unsuccessfully competed with Garvey were often more highly educated and sometimes more aware of the complexity of the problems confronting black people, but the source of their awareness, and often of their prestige, was the white world. Du Bois was the pioneering figure in the Pan-Africanist tradition (which holds that black people everywhere have a common destiny), and his appreciation of Afro-American culture was greater than the foreign-born Garvey's. Yet it was Garvey who received the adulation that black people reserve for those leaders who achieve prominence, even for a time, without white assistance. Du Bois and Garvey are towering figures in twentieth-century black politics, but tragically, they were bitter enemies during their lifetimes and left behind a divided intellectual legacy that has never been completely unified.

Even in Jesse Jackson's campaign there are muted echoes not only of Du Bois's militancy for social change but also of Garvey's visionary racial politics. Although Garvey once asserted that the "vain assumption" that a black man might become President was as futile as "waiting on the devil and his angels" to "direct the affairs of Paradise," he nevertheless called on blacks to "take advantage of every opportunity." Jackson is by no means a black nationalist, but his campaign demonstrates the extent to which nationalist and integrationist themes have become entwined. As President General of the U.N.I.A. and the African Communities' League, Garvey saw Pan-African unity rather than a "rainbow coalition" as his route to power, but it would be a mistake to overlook the similarities between Garvey's calls for racial uplift and Jackson's "I Am Somebody" refrain. Both men came from humble origins and, through strength of will and character, vaulted into leadership over established black leaders from more privileged backgrounds. Both provide powerless blacks with a model of confidence, assertiveness and independence.

If Garvey were alive today, he would doubtless recognize the common elements in his uplift ethic and Jackson's brash, daring political style, his calls for black educational achievement and his use of self-promotion to create an appealing image of success. He would probably appreciate Jackson's effort to create black business opportunities by organizing boycotts. He would sympathize with Jackson's difficulty in gaining the support of the cosmopolitan black elite, while glorying in the fact that both were far more able than their black critics to reach the masses. Garvey would not see Jackson as a fellow nationalist, but he would recognize a leader who, perhaps unconsciously, uses a political vocabulary that reflects the unique experiences and aspirations of black people. Jackson does not have Garvey's organized support, and he may not possess a comparable sense of historical purpose. But he may represent a historical departure that is, in the long term, more significant than Garvey's was.

Once one moves beyond the simplistic notion that black nationalism is merely antiwhite, escapist and violent, it becomes possible to see how its underlying cultural themes have enriched and will continue to enrich American life. The most important outcome of the Jackson campaign may be to introduce racially distinctive political styles into the moribund political system. That Jackson has been able to attract the support of black Baptists and Black Muslims, rural blacks and urban blacks, the politically active and the politically inert, may matter more in the long run than the fact that he has failed to garner the unanimous backing of the black elite, which has historically placed its faith in white liberalism.

Jackson's black critics envy him, much as Du Bois and the educated blacks of the 1920s envied Garvey. With some justification they will claim, as Garvey's critics did, that Jackson's motives are suspect, that his appeal is based partly on demagogy, that his programs are not clearly formulated, that he does not possess the intellectual depth or political experience of other black leaders. Like Garvey, however, Jackson can defend himself by pointing to his indisputable successes. As Garvey demonstrated the widespread receptiveness of blacks to the rhetoric of racial uplift, Jackson has demonstrated that a black political figure need not abandon that rhetoric in order to attract significant white support. Indeed, the rhetoric might be perceived by some whites as an asset rather than a liability. Jackson's success in freeing Lieut. Robert Goodman from Syria certainly depended on luck, but it also demonstrated vividly that black politicians could offer America a difference in cultural perspectives that is useful in a world that is largely nonwhite and non-Western. For better or worse, Jackson may serve as a model for a new generation of black politicians.

The fact that black nationalist themes of racial pride and Pan-Africanist unity can be separated from traditional anti-white animus and racial chauvinism is a measure of the changes that have occurred since Garvey's heyday. During the period after 1921 Garvey attempted to prove to whites that his nationalism did not threaten the social order, but he did it in an opportunistic way that destroyed his credibility. By publicly advocating racial purity and linking himself with white racists, he tried to win favor with whites while neutralizing his black opponents. In 1922, Garvey voiced support for a Mississippi politician's plan to establish an American-sponsored black settler nation in Africa. Instead of strengthening Garvey's position, his meeting with a Ku Klux Klan leader that year narrowed his black support and made him an easier target for J. Edgar Hoover and other government officials. In 1923, Garvey was convicted of illegally using the mails to raise funds for the Black Star Line. After his appeal was turned down in 1925, he entered the Federal penitentiary in Atlanta, where he served almost two years before his sentence was commuted to deportation.

Garvey's rise and fall reveal the strengths and limitations of the black nationalist tradition. Many of its problems stem from the use of the term "black nationalism" to describe a tradition that involves far more than the establishment of a black nation or the migration of blacks to Africa. The idea of a black nation has been an extreme expression of a widely shared desire for black-controlled institutions and for a positive sense of group identity. Garvey and most other important black nationalists saw Africa rather than America as the site for their ambitions, but they also believed in the development of strong African nations as a necessary precondition for black advancement in America.

Like other black nationalists, however, Garvey fell victim to the tendency to seek ideological consistency at the expense of social relevance. He argued that since racism permeates white society, blacks have more to gain from allying themselves with powerful white conservatives than with less powerful white liberals. Similarly, nineteenth-century black nationalist Henry Highland Garnet sought support from the American Colonization Society, which advocated sending free blacks to Africa, and his colleague Martin Delany allied himself with conservative South Carolina Governor Wade Hampton. During the late 1960s the black nationalist leaders who took over the Congress of Racial Equality made their own accommodation with white conservatives in the Nixon Administration.

Yet if black nationalist extremism, like all extremism, has often produced ideologically pure leaders with few followers, it has also been a major source of distinctive political ideas. Unlike the integrationist tradition, which is ideologically rooted in the unrealized ideals of American democracy, the nationalist tradition has sprung from the unique experiences of—to use Malcolm X's phrase—the black victims of American democracy. Integrationists have brought blacks closer to the mainstream; nationalists have insured that they will be able to alter its course. At the peak of his influence, Garvey demonstrated the emotional power of nationalist appeals for racial unity and pride. If his message seems less controversial now, it is because so many of his ideas have become the basic assumptions of black politics. Perhaps the most important of those ideas is that the black racial consciousness produced by white racism is not a curse but a valuable legacy.

~ 1991 ~

All for One and None for All

Adolph Reed Jr.

Adolph Reed Jr., a professor of political science at North-western University and author of *The Jackson Phenomenon*, writes frequently on race and politics for *The Nation*.

JANUARY 28, 1991 ~ The hypocrisy in the white reaction to Louis Farrakhan's "hate-mongering" is transparent. And beneath the platitudes and fatuities about Martin Luther King Jr.'s dream, black Americans are aware of the dual standard governing public outcry. David Duke's racism and anti-Semitism have been more direct and vitriolic than Farrakhan's, but Duke has not provoked comparable public anxiety and denunciation— despite the fact that the ex-Nazi/Klansman has won a seat as a Louisiana State Representative, has run as a "legitimate" candidate for the U.S. Senate and harbors gubernatorial intentions. The heavy metal group Guns n' Roses maintains a repertoire that is unremittingly and unapologetically misogynistic, homophobic, racist and xenophobic, yet the group has escaped the outrage and public censure heaped upon the no more (nor less, certainly) racist and misogynistic Public Enemy. The scurrilous Andrew Dice Clay is granted television specials and a film contract; the no more repugnant 2 Live Crew is censored for obscenity. Recognition of this hypo-critical Jim Crow standard for targeting public scorn naturally breeds resentment and racial defensiveness. The retrograde racial climate fostered by Reaganism particularly stimulates that defensive tendency. It is also rein-forced and cultivated by black elites of all sorts—from the national civil rights advocacy organizations, the Congressional Black Caucus and Jesse Jackson to small-town politicians, journalists and academics, who oppor-tunistically reproduce a political discourse among black citizens that takes race as its only significant category of critical analysis.

Farrakhan has been attacked so vigorously and singularly *in part* because he is black. He is seen by whites as a symbol embodying, and therefore jus-tifying, their fears of a black peril. Blacks have come to his defense *mainly* because he is black and perceived to be a victim of racially inspired defama-tion; he gets points in principle for saying things that antagonize whites.

Few who rally to vindicate him know or have anything substantive to say about his program; most defend him as a strong black voice that whites want to silence. Farrakhan's wager is that he can build a personal following by asserting his apparent victimization as de facto evidence of political legitimacy.

Embracing Farrakhan's image—like wearing an Africa medallion—is an act of vicarious empowerment. More clearly on the campuses but probably outside student life as well, it is a totemic act of the sort distinctive to mass-consumption culture: highly salient but without clear meaning, effortlessly accessible but somehow bestowing in-group status. For college students, inviting Farrakhan forges identity with a power that counterattacks racism and isolation and soothes the anxieties around upward mobility or class maintenance. For non-students, invoking his name forges identity with a power that consoles fleetingly in the face of a marginalized life showing little hope for improvement.

The impetus to invite Farrakhan to speak on campuses is driven by a combination of localized *cri de coeur* and protest, competition and solidarity with black students at other institutions, faddishness and racially mediated adolescent rebelliousness and anxiety. But what happens when he comes? What message does he deliver? What do students hear and how do they receive it? What can that tell us about the depth and meaning of his support?

For many the act of consuming the event is the principal gratification. In that sense going to a Farrakhan speech is identical to going to an M.C. Hammer concert; it is the happening place to be at the moment. Farrakhan is a masterful performer and spellbinding orator. He offers his audience a safely contained catharsis: visceral rebellion without dangerous consequences, an instant, painless inversion of power and status relations. As a talented demagogue, Farrakhan mingles banalities, half-truths, distortions and falsehoods to buttress simplistic and wacky theories. The result is a narrative in which he takes on the role of racial conscience and, in Malcolm's old phrase, "tells it like it is." He cajoles, berates, exhorts, instructs and consoles—all reassuringly, without upsetting the framework of conservative petit-bourgeois convention.

Indeed, Farrakhan has reproduced the contradiction within the old canon of Islam, the tension between militant posture and conservative program. But that contradiction fits the ambivalent position of the student audience. Their racial militancy often rests atop basically conventional, if not conservative, aspirations: for example, the desire to penetrate—or create black-controlled alternatives to—the "glass ceiling" barring access to the upper reaches of corporate wealth and power. Radical rhetoric is attractive when it speaks to their frustrations as members of a minority, as long as it does not conflict with their hopes for corporate success and belief in their own superiority to a benighted black "underclass."

The combination of cathartic, feel-good militancy and conservative substance is the source as well of whatever comparable following Farrakhan may have generated among the older population. It is also what makes him a dangerous force in American life—quite apart from what he thinks of whites in general or Jews in particular. He weds a radical, oppositional style to a program that proposes private and individual responses to social problems; he endorses moral repressiveness; he asserts racial essentialism; he affirms male authority; and he lauds bootstrap capitalism. In defining his and the Nation's role as bringing the holy word to a homogeneous but defective population, moreover, he has little truck for cultivation of democratic debate among Afro-Americans, and he is quick to castigate black critics with the threatening language of race treason.

To Farrakhan the most pressing problems confronting the poor and working-class Afro-American population are not poverty and dispossession themselves but their putative behavioral and attitudinal byproducts: drugs, crime, social "pathology." In an August interview in *Emerge* he declared that to improve black Americans' condition it is necessary first to "recognize that we as a people are sick." In his March 13, 1990, *Donahue* appearance he maintained that blacks suffer from a dependent, welfare mentality inculcated in slavery; there and elsewhere (in a March 1, 1990, *Washington Post* interview, for example) he has implicitly trivialized and challenged the propriety of the Thirteenth Amendment, alleging that at Emancipation the infantilized blacks "didn't have the mentality of a free people to go and do for ourselves." (In this view Farrakhan echoes not only Daniel Patrick Moynihan's notorious 1965 report on the black family but also much older racist representations: the common belief in the early twentieth century that emancipated blacks would die out because of their incompetence at independent life in civilized society and the antebellum view that justified slavery as a humanitarian service for childlike savages who could not exist independently.)

Farrakhan romanticizes the segregation era as a time of black business success and laments that "throughout the South the economic advancement that we gained under Jim Crow is literally dead." He suggested in *Emerge* that civil rights legislation has done black citizens general harm because "women, gays, lesbians and Jews have taken advantage of civil rights laws, antidiscrimination laws, housing laws, and they have marched on to a better life while the people who made it happen are going farther and farther behind economically." He proposed the "real solution" in a very sympathetic July 23, 1990, interview in *The Spotlight*, organ of the ultra-reactionary Liberty Lobby:

If I am sick and I'm a member of your household and I have a communicable disease, what you do (so that the disease does not affect the whole family), you remove me from the house and you put me in a place which is separate to allow me to come back to health. Then I can return to my family. Here, when people have been under oppression for 400 years, it produces an ill effect. . . . You have . . . millions of [Black] people who are out of it in terms of our ability to take advantage of even the laws that are on the books right now. We are not creating jobs for ourselves. We are sitting in a dependent posture waiting for white people to create a job for us. And if you don't create a job for us we threaten to picket or wait on welfare to come.

Farrakhan's views of politics and government also share significant features with the Reaganite right. The flip side of his self-help notion is rejection of government responsibility for the welfare of the citizenry. The highly touted Muslim "Dopebusters" drug program in Washington's Mayfair Mansions (where I lived as a child, incidentally) is, after all, advertised as a case of successful privatization. Predictably, Farrakhan shows little regard for the state's integrity as a secular institution. In announcing the Nation's foray into running candidates for public office (for the Washington school board and two Congressional seats, one of them contested by Dr. Abdul Alim Muhammad of Dopebusters fame), he maintained in the Nation's organ, *The Final Call*, that politics needs "somebody trained in divine law, then trained in the law of the land" and announced that the Nation of Islam has been "given by Allah the right guidance for our people and the right guidance for our nation." Like Reagan, he assumes the classic demagogic tack of an antipolitical politics, presenting himself and his subalterns as redeemers coming from outside the political realm and untainted by its corruptions. Their mission is to bring moral order.

How can it be that Farrakhan's actual vision of and for black America has been so noncontroversial? Why have the civil rights establishment and other liberal black opinion leaders not publicly expressed more vocal concern about its protofascist nature and substance? Some of the reticence may derive from fear of being attacked for race disloyalty, but the black petit-bourgeois chorus of praise for the Nation's rhetoric of self-help and moral rearmament reveals a deeper reason for the absence of criticism. The same repugnant, essentially Victorian view of the inner-city black poor as incompetent and morally defective that undergirds Farrakhan's agenda suffuses the political discourse of the black petite bourgeoisie. That view informs the common sense, moreover, even of many of those identified with the left. Of course, not many would admit to the level of contempt that Farrakhan has expressed publicly:

> Not one of you [*Spotlight* editorial staff] would mind, maybe, my living next door to you, because I'm a man of a degree of intelligence, of moral character. I'm not a wild, partying fellow. I'm not a noisemaker. I keep my home very clean and my lawn very nice. . . . With some of us who have learned how to act at home and abroad, you might not have problems. . . . Drive through the ghettoes, and see our people. See how we live. Tell me that you want your son or daughter to marry one of these. No, you won't.

In sum, Louis Farrakhan has become prominent in the public eye because he appeals symbolically both to black frustration and alienation in this retrograde era and to white racism, disingenuousness and naïveté. He also responds to the status anxiety, paternalistic class prejudice and ideological conservatism embedded within black petit-bourgeois race militancy. His antiwhite or anti-Semitic views are neither the most important issue surrounding Farrakhan nor the greatest reason for concern about his prospects for growing influence. After all, he will never be able to impose his beliefs—no matter how obnoxious or heinous—on any group of white Americans. More significant, and more insidious, is the fact that racial units are his essential categories for defining and comprehending political life. That fact obviously establishes him on common conceptual ground with all manner of racists. (*The Spotlight* was happily curious about whether he and David Duke actually would disagree on anything in a debate rumored to be in the works.)

His racial essentialism has an appeal for many blacks in a purely demagogic way. It also gives him an outlook that seems disarmingly sensible to whites—at least those who can overlook his fiery pro-black sentiments and devil theories—because it fits into the hoary "What do your people want?" framework for discussing black Americans. That essentialist outlook also underlies his self-help rhetoric, which appeals to both whites and middle-class blacks. Whites like it because it implies that blacks should pull themselves up by their bootstraps and not make demands on government. Middle-class blacks like it because it legitimizes a "special role" for the black petite bourgeoisie over the benighted remainder of the race. In both views, "self-help" with respect to ordinary black Americans replaces a standard expectation of democratic citizenship—a direct, unmediated relation to the institutions and processes of public authority. Self-help ideology is a form of privatization and therefore implies cession of the principle that government is responsible for improving the lives of the citizenry and advancing egalitarian interests; it also rests on a premise that black Americans cannot effectively make demands on the state directly as citizens but must go through intermediaries constituted as guardians of collective racial self-interest. Ironically, "self-help" requires dissolution of the autonomous civic self of Afro-Americans.

The link between self-help rhetoric and racial custodianship is as old as Booker T. Washington, the model of organic racial leadership Farrakhan articulates. The idea that black racial interests can be embodied in a single individual has always been attractively economical for white elites. Giving Washington a railroad car for his own use to avoid Jim Crow was a lot cheaper for white elites and less disruptive than socioeconomic democratization and preservation of citizenship rights. Jesse Jackson updated the claim to organic racial leadership and brokerage by enlisting mass media technology to legitimize it, and Farrakhan is following in Jackson's steps. Because of his organization and ideology, however, Farrakhan more than his predecessors throws into relief the dangerous, fascistic presumptions inscribed at the foundation of that model. That—underscored by the brownshirt character of the Fruit of Islam and the history of the old Nation during Farrakhan's ascent—is what makes him uniquely troubling. But demonizing him misses the point; it is the idea of organic representation of the racial collectivity that makes him possible.

It is that idea, whether expressed flamboyantly by Farrakhan or in the more conventional petit-bourgeois synecdoche that folds all black interests into a narrow class agenda, that most needs to be repudiated. Its polluting and demobilizing effects on Afro-American political life have never been more visible, thanks to promotion by the mass media's special combination of racist cynicism and gullibility. Cheap hustlers and charlatans, corrupt and irresponsible public officials and perpetrators of any sort of fraud can manipulate the generic defensiveness decreed by a politics of organic racial representation to support their scams or sidestep their guilt—all too often for offenses against black constituents. A straight line connects Washington's Tuskegee Machine, which sought to control access to philanthropic support for racial agendas, to Jackson's insinuation that "respect" for him is respect for all black Americans to Farrakhan's death threat against Milton Coleman to the pathetic specter of the rouges' gallery of Farrakhan, Illinois Representative Gus Savage, the Rev. Al Sharpton, the Rev. George Stallings and Tawana Brawley sharing the stage with Marion Barry at a rally to defend the corrupt Mayor's honor. That image captures the depth of crisis of political vision that racial organicism has wrought.

~ 1991 ~

Grand Marshall

Randall Kennedy

Randall Kennedy, a professor at Harvard Law School and editor of *Reconstruction*, worked as a law clerk for Justice Thurgood Marshall.

August 12/19, 1991 ~ My father once told me that when he ventured into a Southern courthouse years ago to hear Thurgood Marshall argue a voting rights case, he was so afraid of seeming "uppity" that he pretended to be the janitor—and so inspired by Marshall's performance that he will always consider him "the biggest, baddest and boldest man in the world."

I had the great privilege of working for Justice Thurgood Marshall as a law clerk in 1983-84. He was a stern and exacting taskmaster who told you bluntly (and in front of your co-clerks) if he thought your work was beneath his standards and offered praise only sparingly. A memo on which he wrote "OK" remains a dear possession. He didn't stand on ceremony or demand that his ego be stroked. He didn't seem to care, for instance, how he was addressed by his staff. Some clerks called him "Justice Marshall," others simply "Judge." At moments of high anxiety, I called him "Boss." His informality led me, like many observers, occasionally to underestimate him. Every time I did—once, for instance, I tried to grind my own ax in the draft of an opinion—he proved me wrong, demonstrating the knowledge and devotion to duty that have made him one of the great figures of American law.

In the many farewells to Marshall two points about his career have been obscured. One is that for most of his tenure he fought against a conservative majority on the Court. When Marshall was elevated to the Court in 1967, he joined not a den of judicial revolutionaries but a set of establishment lawyers whose sober reformism rarely ventured beyond nullifying the most blatant affronts to national ideals. Moreover, not long after Marshall arrived, the Court's liberal wing began to disintegrate; by 1975 Earl Warren, Abe Fortas, Hugo Black and William Douglas had all been replaced by the appointees of Richard Nixon and Gerald Ford. An outsider during all those many years when he faced the Court as the nation's foremost civil rights attorney, he remained something of an outsider even after his ascension to the nation's highest tribunal.

Yet, and here is the second point that is often overlooked, Marshall succeeded in significantly influencing the Court. A good example is his campaign to limit, if not abolish, peremptory challenges—acts by which attorneys dismiss potential jurors without offering reasons. In 1965, in *Swain v. Alabama*, a 5-to-4 majority denied a black defendant accused of raping a white woman the right to examine the white prosecutor's use of peremptory challenges, even though the prosecutor struck all the blacks who might have served on the jury in a county that was at least 25 percent black and in which no black had served on a trial jury for fifteen years. Essentially, the Court held that prosecutors could exclude potential jurors on the basis of race so long as they did so as a matter of trial tactics. *Swain* became, as one commentator put it, the constitutional blueprint for the perpetuation of the all-white jury.

Describing the racist misuse of peremptory challenges as "one of the gravest and most persistent problems facing the American judiciary," Marshall began in 1982 to write dissents from denials of certiorari—rulings in which the Court, without explanation, declines to hear a case—whenever the case would have compelled a decision on the viability of *Swain*. His withering criticisms encouraged defense attorneys and lower court judges either to evade or to attack *Swain*, and his persistence set into motion a chain of events that led to its demise.

Justice Marshall's successful campaign to overturn *Swain* drew upon knowledge of two areas of law about which he is particularly concerned and knowledgeable: equal protection and criminal procedure. It would be a mistake, however, to view Marshall as a parochial jurist who was good for addressing only a narrow band of legal issues. Because conservative Chief Justices sought to prevent him from writing opinions for the Court in major cases involving large, controversial matters, he was often given the task of writing opinions in arcane, highly technical and decidedly nonglamorous corners of the law. Thus he wrote many fine opinions interpreting federal income tax statutes and untangling complex railroad legislation, displaying a degree of lawyerly competence that commentators have failed to appreciate sufficiently.

Having said that, we shall miss him most in the great political areas of the law. We shall miss him as the Court narrows and perhaps wholly jettisons the constitutional right to sexual and reproductive privacy; as it deregulates capital punishment, mangling long-established doctrines in the process; as it continues to interpret statutes and the Constitution in ways that show inadequate solicitude for racial minorities, women, gays and lesbians, the handicapped, the economically impoverished and all other vulnerable people.

Near the end of my clerkship, I asked Justice Marshall whether he felt discouraged by trends that pushed him increasingly to the margins of the Court's jurisprudence. He told me that he did not, that he was too busy to be discouraged. He suggested that progressives seeking to create a more just society had better stay busy too. It remains good advice from a great man who deserves our gratitude.

Chapter Four

~

VOICES

W. E. B. DuBois

January 25, 1958 by Berger

~ 1866 ~
The Liberator Released
Octavius Brooks Frothingham

In 1866, *The Nation*—itself founded by a group of abolitionists—paid tribute to the final issue of William Lloyd Garrison's fiery anti-slavery newspaper, *The Liberator*. Octavius Brooks Frothingham was a minister and author of several biographies on prominent abolitionists.

January 4, 1866 ~ *The Liberator*, representative of the original abolitionists, has deceased, or rather has been translated; for its end was not so much an extinction as a disappearance in the light which it heralded and helped to bring in. It expired last Friday in the arms of victory. The Constitutional Amendment, which declared that slavery no longer existed in the United States, was publicly ratified in season to be duly announced and welcomed in the issue of December 22, Forefather's Day, leaving the last issue free for the final words of memory and jubilation. The paper has finished its course because it has reached its goal; but if its goal had been set a century further on, nothing would have finished its course till the goal had been reached; for it was supported by its principle; it lived on its nerve. If want of money could have killed it, the paper would have been starved out long ago. If hate and loathing could have destroyed it, it would not have lived a twelve-month. All the packs were in full cry after it the instant it was discovered, and it seemed a very small thing to kill. A more insignificant enemy than it looked to be thirty-five years ago it would be hard to imagine. We have before us, as we write, the first number of the paper, published in Boston, at No. 6 Merchants' Hall, January 1, 1831. The sheet is a span and a half long and a span wide. The editor declares that he will be "as harsh as truth and as

uncompromising as justice;" that he is in earnest, that he will not equivocate, that he will not excuse, that he will not retreat a single inch, and that
he will be heard. The publishers, on their part, proclaim their determination
"to print the paper as long as they can subsist on bread and water, or their
hands can find employment." The paper has not much more than doubled
its size since then; but steadily, week by week, never failing in a single
instance to come to time, it has dropped its water upon the nation's marble
heart. Its tenacity has been as wonderful as its intensity. The abolition of
chattel slavery was its aim, and it never for a moment lost sight of it. There
was a stern monotony in its issues that was like the pressure of fate. It was
an unvarying soliloquy thirty-five years long. Line upon line, precept upon
precept, was its rule and method. Other matters found place in its columns
but they never distracted attention from this. The poetry was somewhat
lacking in poetic art, but it was all inspired by anti-slavery conviction. The
literary criticism was not delicate, but it was always honest and earnest.
Many of the contributions were rough in style and crude in thought, but
they were contributions to the main cause. Every strange reform found a
voice in its columns, but their currents came in as tributary streams to swell
the tide of moral sentiment which was to carry away the one gigantic wrong
of slavery. The editor, from year to year, kept his pledge—he never did
equivocate, excuse, or retreat. He knew no distinction of persons; he knew
no difference of times or seasons. Justice does not vary with policies or
events. Other newspapers might change hands and principles; parties swung
round to opposite sides; great political issues appeared and disappeared;
statesmen filled the public eye and vanished; cabinets went in and out;
administrations rose and fell; elections again and again convulsed the country and altered the old sea margins of opinion. The editor of *The Liberator*
never took his eye from the slave nor cared where other men fixed their
eyes, save as they smiled or frowned on the slave. It is, perhaps, the most
remarkable instance on record of single-hearted devotion to a cause.

~ 1926 ~

The Negro Artist and the Racial Mountain

Langston Hughes

In 1926, the Harlem Renaissance was in full flower; the poet Langston Hughes was one of its central figures. In this essay, Hughes urges black intellectuals and artists to break free of the artificial standards set for them by whites.

June 23, 1926 ~ One of the most promising of the young Negro poets said to me once, "I want to be a poet—not a Negro poet," meaning, I believe, "I want to write like a white poet"; meaning subconsciously, "I would like to be a white poet"; meaning behind that, "I would like to be white." And I was sorry the young man said that, for no great poet has ever been afraid of being himself. And I doubted then that, with his desire to run away spiritually from his race, this boy would ever be a great poet. But this is the mountain standing in the way of any true Negro art in America—this urge within the race toward whiteness, the desire to pour racial individuality into the mold of American standardization, and to be as little Negro and as much American as possible.

But let us look at the immediate background of this young poet. His family is of what I suppose one would call the Negro middle class: people who are by no means rich yet never uncomfortable nor hungry—smug, contented, respectable folk, members of the Baptist church. The father goes to work every morning. He is a chief steward at a large white club. The mother sometimes does fancy sewing or supervises parties for the rich families of the town. The children go to a mixed school. In the home they read white papers and magazines. And the mother often says "Don't be like niggers" when the children are bad. A frequent phrase from the father is, "Look how well a white man does things." And so the word white comes to be unconsciously a symbol of all the virtues. It holds for the children beauty, morality, and money. The whisper of "I want to be white" runs silently through their minds. This young poet's home is, I believe, a fairly typical home of the colored middle class. One sees immediately how difficult it would be for an artist born in such a home to interest himself in interpreting the beauty of his own people. He is never taught to see that beauty. He is taught rather not to see it, or if he does, to be ashamed of it when it is not according to Caucasian patterns.

For racial culture the home of a self-styled "high-class" Negro has nothing better to offer. Instead there will perhaps be more aping of things white than in a less cultured or less wealthy home. The father is perhaps a doctor, lawyer, landowner, or politician. The mother may be a social worker, or a teacher, or she may do nothing and have a maid. Father is often dark but he has usually married the lightest woman he could find. The family attend a fashionable church where few really colored faces are to be found. And they themselves draw a color line. In the North they go to white theaters and white movies. And in the South they have at least two cars and a house "like white folks." Nordic manners, Nordic faces, Nordic hair, Nordic art (if any), and an Episcopal heaven. A very high mountain indeed for the would-be racial artist to climb in order to discover himself and his people.

But then there are the low-down folks, the so-called common element, and they are the majority—may the Lord be praised! The people who have their nip of gin on Saturday nights and are not too important to themselves or the community, or too well fed, or too learned to watch the lazy world go round. They live on Seventh Street in Washington or State Street in Chicago and they do not particularly care whether they are like white folks or anybody else. Their joy runs, bang! into ecstasy. Their religion soars to a shout. Work maybe a little today, rest a little tomorrow. Play awhile. Sing awhile. O, let's dance! These common people are not afraid of spirituals, as for a long time their more intellectual brethren were, and jazz is their child. They furnish a wealth of colorful, distinctive material for any artist because they still hold their own individuality in the face of American standardizations. And perhaps these common people will give to the world its truly great Negro artist, the one who is not afraid to be himself. Whereas the better-class Negro would tell the artist what to do, the people at least let him alone when he does appear. And they are not ashamed of him—if they know he exists at all. And they accept what beauty is their own without question.

Certainly there is, for the American Negro artist who can escape the restrictions the more advanced among his own group would put upon him, a great field of unused material ready for his art. Without going outside his race, and even among the better classes with their "white" culture and conscious American manners, but still Negro enough to be different, there is sufficient matter to furnish a black artist with a lifetime of creative work. And when he chooses to touch on the relations between Negroes and whites in this country with their innumerable overtones and undertones, surely, and especially for literature and the drama, there is an inexhaustible supply of themes at hand. To these the Negro artist can give his racial individuality, his heritage of rhythm and warmth, and his incongruous humor that so often, as in the Blues, becomes ironic laughter mixed with tears. But let us look again at the mountain.

A prominent Negro clubwoman in Philadelphia paid eleven dollars to hear Raquel Meller sing Andalusian popular songs. But she told me a few weeks before she would not think of going to hear "that woman," Clara Smith, a great black artist, sing Negro folk songs. And many an upper-class Negro church, even now, would not dream of employing a spiritual in its services. The drab melodies in white folks' hymnbooks are much to be preferred. "We want to worship the Lord correctly and quietly. We don't believe in 'shouting.' Let's be dull like the Nordics," they say, in effect.

The road for the serious black artist, then, who would produce a racial art is most certainly rocky and the mountain is high. Until recently he received almost no encouragement for his work from either white or colored people. The fine novels of Chestnutt go out of print with neither race noticing their passing. The quaint charm and humor of Dunbar's dialect verse brought to him, in his day, largely the same kind of encouragement one would give a sideshow freak (A colored man writing poetry! How odd!) or a clown (How amusing!).

The present vogue in things Negro, although it may do as much harm as good for the budding colored artist, has at least done this: it has brought him forcibly to the attention of his own people among whom for so long, unless the other race had noticed him beforehand, he was a prophet with little honor. I understand that Charles Gilpin acted for years in Negro theaters without any special acclaim from his own, but when Broadway gave him eight curtain calls, Negroes, too, began to beat a tin pan in his honor. I know a young colored writer, a manual worker by day, who had been writing well for the colored magazines for some years, but it was not until he recently broke into the white publications and his first book was accepted by a prominent New York publisher that the "best" Negroes in his city took the trouble to discover that he lived there. Then almost immediately they decided to give a grand dinner for him. But the society ladies were careful to whisper to his mother that perhaps she'd better not come. They were not sure she would have an evening gown.

The Negro artist works against an undertow of sharp criticism and misunderstanding from his own group and unintentional bribes from the whites. "O, be respectable, write about nice people, show how good we are," say the Negroes. "Be stereotyped, don't go too far, don't shatter our illusions about you, don't amuse us too seriously. We will pay you," say the whites. Both would have told Jean Toomer not to write "Cane." The colored people did not praise it. The white people did not buy it. Most of the colored people who did read "Cane" hate it. They are afraid of it. Although the critics gave it good reviews the public remained indifferent. Yet (excepting the work of Du Bois) "Cane" contains the finest prose written by a Negro in America. And like the singing of Robeson, it is truly racial.

But in spite of the Nordicized Negro intelligentsia and the desires of some white editors we have an honest American Negro literature already with us. Now I await the rise of the Negro theater. Our folk music, having achieved world-wide fame, offers itself to the genius of the great individual American Negro composer who is to come. And within the next decade I expect to see the work of a growing school of colored artists who paint and model the beauty of dark faces and create with new technique the expressions of their own soul-world. And the Negro dancers who will dance like flame and the singers who will continue to carry our songs to all who listen—they will be with us in even greater numbers tomorrow.

Most of my own poems are racial in theme and treatment, derived from the life I know. In many of them I try to grasp and hold some of the meanings and rhythms of jazz. I am sincere as I know how to be in these poems and yet after every reading I answer questions like these from my own people: Do you think Negroes should always write about Negroes? I wish you wouldn't read some of your poems to white folks. How do you find anything interesting in a place like a cabaret? Why do you write about black people? You aren't black. What makes you do so many jazz poems?

But jazz to me is one of the inherent expressions of Negro life in America: the eternal tom-tom beating in the Negro soul—the tom-tom of revolt against weariness in a white world, a world of subway trains, and work, work, work; the tom-tom of joy and laughter, and pain swallowed in a smile. Yet the Philadelphia clubwoman is ashamed to say that her race created it and she does not like me to write about it. The old subconscious "white is best" runs through her mind. Years of study under white teachers, a lifetime of white books, pictures, and papers, and white manners, morals, and Puritan standards made her dislike the spirituals. And now she turns up her nose at jazz and all its manifestations—likewise almost everything else distinctly racial. She doesn't care for the Winold Reiss portraits of Negroes because they are "too Negro." She does not want a true picture of herself from anybody. She wants the artist to flatter her, to make the white world believe that all Negroes are as smug and as near white in soul as she wants to be. But, to my mind, it is the duty of the younger Negro artist, if he accepts any duties at all from outsiders, to change through the force of his art that old whispering "I want to be white," hidden in the aspirations of his people, to "Why should I want to be white? I am a Negro—and beautiful!"

So I am ashamed for the black poet who says, "I want to be a poet, not a Negro poet," as though his own racial world were not as interesting as any other world. I am ashamed, too, for the colored artist who runs from the painting of Negro faces to the painting of sunsets after the manner of the academicians because he fears the strange un-whiteness of his own features. An artist must be free to choose what he does, certainly, but he must also never be afraid to do what he might choose.

Let the blare of Negro jazz bands and the bellowing voice of Bessie Smith singing Blues penetrate the closed ears of the colored near-intellectuals until they listen and perhaps understand. Let Paul Robeson singing Water Boy, and Rudolph Fisher writing about the streets of Harlem, and Jean Toomer holding the heart of Georgia in his hands, and Aaron Douglas drawing strange black fantasies cause the smug Negro middle class to turn from their white, respectable, ordinary books and papers to catch a glimmer of their own beauty. We younger Negro artists who create now intend to express our individual dark-skinned selves without fear or shame. If white people are pleased we are glad. If they are not, it doesn't matter. We know we are beautiful. And ugly too. The tom-tom cries and the tom-tom laughs. If colored people are pleased we are glad. If they are not, their displeasure doesn't matter either. We build our temples for tomorrow, strong as we know how, and we stand on top of the mountain, free within ourselves.

~ 1956 ~

Why I Won't Vote

W.E.B. Du Bois

In 1956, *The Nation* invited several writers and activists to comment on the upcoming presidential election, which pitted incumbent Dwight D. Eisenhower against Democratic challenger Adlai Stevenson.

October 20, 1956 ~ In 1956, I shall not go to the polls. I have not registered. I believe that democracy has so far disappeared in the United States that no "two evils" exist. There is but one evil party with two names, and it will be elected despite all I can do or say. There is no third party. On the Presidential ballot in a few states (seventeen in 1952), a "Socialist" Party will appear. Few will hear its appeal because it will have almost no opportunity to take part in the campaign and explain its platform. If a voter organizes or advocates a real third-party movement, he may be accused of seeking to overthrow this government by "force and violence." Anything he advocates by way of significant reform will be called "Communist" and will of necessity be Communist in the sense that it must advocate such things as government ownership of the means of production; government in business; the limitation of private profit; social medicine, government housing and federal aid to education; the total abolition of race bias; and the welfare state. These things are on every Communist program; these things are the aim of socialism. Any American who advocates them today, no matter how sincerely, stands in danger of losing his job, surrendering his social status and perhaps landing in jail. The witnesses against him may be liars or insane or criminals. These witnesses need give no proof for their charges and may not even be known or appear in person. They may be in the pay of the United States Government. A.D.A.s and "Liberals" are not third parties; they seek to act as tails to kites. But since the kites are self-propelled and radar-controlled, tails are quite superfluous and rather silly.

The present Administration is carrying on the greatest preparation for war in the history of mankind. Stevenson promises to maintain or increase this effort. The weight of our taxation is unbearable and rests mainly and deliberately on the poor. This Administration is dominated and directed by wealth and for the accumulation of wealth. It runs smoothly like a well-organized industry and *should* do so because industry runs it for the benefit of industry.

The "other" party has surrendered all party differences in foreign affairs, and foreign affairs are our most important affairs today and take most of our taxes. Even in domestic affairs, how does Stevenson differ from Eisenhower? He uses better English than Dulles, thank God! He has a sly humor, where Eisenhower has none. Beyond this Stevenson stands on the race question in the South not far from where his grandfather Adlai stood sixty-three years ago, which reconciles him to the South. He has no clear policy on war or preparation for war; on water and flood control; on reduction of taxation; on the welfare state. He wavers on civil rights and his party blocked civil rights in the Senate until Douglas of Illinois admitted that the Democratic Senate would and could stop even the right of Senators to vote. Douglas had a right to complain. Three million voters sent him to the Senate to speak for them. His voice was drowned and his voice nullified by Eastland, the chairman of the Senate Judiciary Committee, who was elected by 151,000 voters. This is the democracy in the United States which we peddle abroad.

Negroes hope to muster 400,000 votes in 1956. Where will they cast them? What have the Republicans done to enforce the education decision of the Supreme Court? What they advertised as fair employment was exactly nothing, and Nixon was just the man to explain it. What has the Administration done to rescue Negro workers, the most impoverished group in the nation, half of whom receive less than half the median wage of the nation, while the nation sends billions abroad to protect oil investments and help employ slave labor in the Union of South Africa and the Rhodesias? Very well, and will the party of Talmadge, Eastland and Ellender do better than the Republicans if the Negroes return them to office?

I have no advice for others in this election. Are you voting Democratic? Well and good; all I ask is why? Are you voting for Eisenhower and his smooth team of bright ghostwriters? Again, why? Will your helpless vote either way support or restore democracy to America?

Is the answer the election of 1956? We can make a sick man President and set him to a job which would strain a man in robust health. So he dies, and what do we get to lead us? With Stevenson and Nixon, with Eisenhower and Eastland, we remain in the same mess. I will be no party to it and that will make little difference. You will take large part and bravely march to the polls, and that also will make no difference. Stop running Russia and giving Chinese advise when we cannot rule ourselves decently.

Stop yelling about a democracy we do not have. Democracy is dead in the United States. Yet there is still nothing to replace real democracy. Drop the chains, then, that bind our brains. Drive the money-changers from the seats of the Cabinet and the halls of Congress. Call back some faint spirit of Jefferson and Lincoln, and when again we can hold a fair election on real issues, let's vote, and not till then. Is this impossible? Then democracy in America is impossible.

~ 1965 ~
"Let Justice Roll Down"
Martin Luther King Jr.

From 1961 to 1966, the Reverend Martin Luther King Jr. wrote an annual essay for *The Nation* on the state of civil rights and race relations in America.

March 15, 1965 ~ When 1963 came to a close, more than a few skeptical voices asked what substantial progress had been achieved through the demonstrations that had drawn more than a million Negroes into the streets. By the close of 1964, the pessimistic clamor was stilled by the music of major victories. Taken together, the two years marked a historic turning point for the civil rights movement; in the previous century no comparable change for the Negro had occurred. Now, even the most cynical acknowledged that at Birmingham, as at Concord, a shot had been fired that was heard around the world.

Before examining 1964 in greater depth, some comment is necessary on the events currently unfolding in Alabama. After the passage of the Civil Rights Act and with the defeat of Barry Goldwater, there was widespread expectation that barriers would disintegrate with swift inevitability. This easy optimism could not survive the first test. In the hard-core states of the South, while some few were disposed to accommodate, the walls remained erect and reinforced. That was to be expected, for the basic institutions of government, commerce, industry and social patterns in the South all rest upon the embedded institution of segregation. Change is not accomplished by peeling off superficial layers when the causes are rooted deeply in the heart of the organism.

Those who expected a cheap victory in a climate of complacency were shocked into reality by Selma and Marion, Ala. In Selma, the position was implacable resistance. At one point, ten times as many Negroes were in jail as were on the registration rolls. Out of 15,000 eligible to vote, less than 350 were registered.

Selma involves more than disenfranchisement. Its inner texture reveals overt and covert forms of terror and intimidation—that uniquely Southern form of existence for Negroes in which life is a constant state of acute

defensiveness and deprivation. Yet if Selma outrages democratic sensibili-
ties, neighboring Wilcox County offers something infinitely worse. Sheriff
P.C. Jenkins has held office in Wilcox for twenty-six years. He is a local
legend because when he wants a Negro for a crime, he merely sends out
word and the Negro comes in to be arrested. This is intimidation and
degradation reminiscent only of chattel slavery. This is white supremacist
arrogance and Negro servility possible only in an atmosphere where the
Negro feels himself so isolated, so hopeless, that he is stripped of all dignity. And as if they were in competition to obliterate the United States
Constitution within Alabama's borders state troopers only a few miles away
clubbed and shot Negro demonstrators in Marion.

Are demonstrations of any use, some ask, when resistance is so unyielding?
Would the slower processes of legislation and law enforcement ultimately
accomplish greater results more painlessly? Demonstrations, experience has
shown, are part of the process of stimulating legislation and law enforcement. The federal government reacts to events more quickly when a situation of conflict cries out for its intervention. Beyond this, demonstrations
have a creative effect on the social and psychological climate that is not
matched by the legislative process. Those who have lived under the corro-
sive humiliation of daily intimidation are imbued by demonstrations with a
sense of courage and dignity that strengthens their personalities. Through
demonstrations, Negroes learn that unity and militance have more force
than bullets. They find that the bruises of clubs, electric cattle prods and
fists hurt less than the scars of submission. And segregationists learn from
demonstrations that Negroes who have been taught to fear can also be
taught to be fearless. Finally, the millions of Americans on the sidelines
learn that inhumanity wears an official badge and wields the power of law in
large areas of the democratic nation of their pride.

In addition to these ethical and psychological considerations, our work in
the black-belt counties of Alabama has enabled us to develop further a tactical pattern whose roots extend back to Birmingham and Montgomery. Our
movement has from the earliest days of SCLC adhered to a method which
uses nonviolence in a special fashion. We have consistently operated on the
basis of total community involvement. It is manifestly easier to initiate
actions with a handful of dedicated supporters, but we have sought to make
activists of all our people, rather than draw some activists from the mass.
    Our militant elements were used, not as small striking detachments, but
to organize. Through them, and by patient effort, we have attempted to
involve Negroes from industry, the land, the home, the professions;
Negroes of advanced age, middle age, youth and the very young. In Birm-

ingham, Montgomery, Selma, St. Augustine and elsewhere, when we marched it was as a community, not as a small and unimpressive, if symbolic, assemblage. The charge that we were outside agitators, devoid of support from contented local Negroes, could not be convincing when the procession of familiar local faces could be seen block after block in solid array.

The second element in our tactics after Montgomery was to formulate demands that covered varied aspects of Negro life. If voting campaigns or lunch-counter sit-ins appeared central in press reports, they were but a part of our broader aims. In Birmingham, employment opportunity was a demand pressed as forcefully as desegregation of public facilities. In Selma, our four points encompass voting rights, employment opportunities, improved interracial communication and paved streets in the Negro neighborhoods. The last demand may appear to Northerners to lack some of the historic importance of voting rights. To the Southern Negro the fact that anyone can identify where the ghetto begins by noting where the pavement ends is one of the many offensive experiences in his life. The neighborhood is degraded to degrade the person in it.

The Mississippi Summer Project of the combined civil rights organizations was accorded the traditional Mississippi welcome of murder, arson and terror, and persisted under fire until even the Klan recognized that its sanctuary had been overrun. The isolated Negroes of that state were drawn into the vibrant national struggle. To mark their new status they formed a political party whose voice was heard loudly and clearly at the Democratic National convention and in the Congress.

But perhaps the most significant development of 1963 and 1964 was the emergence of a disciplined, perceptive Negro electorate, almost 100 per cent larger than that of the 1960 Presidential election. Mississippi, the Civil Rights Act, and the new massive Negro vote each represents a particular form of struggle; nevertheless, they are interrelated. Together, they signify the new ability of the movement to function simultaneously in varied arenas, and with varied methods.

Each accomplishment was the culmination of long years of ache and agony. The new Negro vote best illustrates this point. Quietly, without the blare of trumpets, without marching legions to excite the spirit, thousands of patient, persistent Negroes worked day in and day out, laboriously adding one name to another in the registration books. Finally on November 7, in an electoral confrontation vitally important to their existence, they displayed the power which had long been accumulating. On the following day every political expert knew that a mature and permanent Negro electorate had emerged. A powerful, unified political force had come into being.

While elsewhere electioneering was being conducted systematically, another detachment was assaulting the fortress walls of Mississippi, long immune to the discipline of justice. As the confrontation boiled and seethed even in remote rural counties, the revulsion of decent Americans mounted. The wanton burning of churches, the inexpressibly cruel murder of young civil rights workers, not only failed to paralyze the movement; they became a grisly and eloquent demonstration to the whole nation of the moral degeneracy upon which segregation rests.

The Civil Rights Act was expected by many to suffer the fate of the Supreme Court decisions on school desegregation. In particular, it was thought that the issue of public accommodations would encounter massive defiance. But this pessimism overlooked a factor of supreme importance. The legislation was not a product of charity of white America for a supine black America, nor was it the result of enlightened leadership by the judiciary. This legislation was first written in the streets. The epic thrust of the millions of Negroes who demonstrated in 1963 in hundreds of cities won strong white allies to the cause. Together, they created a "coalition of conscience" which awoke a hitherto somnolent Congress. The legislation was polished and refined in the marble halls of Congress, but the vivid marks of its origins in the turmoil of mass meetings and marches were on it, and the vigor and momentum of its turbulent birth carried past the voting and insured substantial compliance.

Apart from its own provisions, the new law stimulated and focused attention on economic needs. An assault on poverty was planned in 1964, and given preliminary and experimental shape.

The fusing of economic measures with civil rights needs; the boldness to penetrate every region of the Old South; the undergirding of the whole by the massive Negro vote, both North and South, all place the freedom struggle on a new elevated level.

The old tasks of awakening the Negro to motion while educating America to the miseries of Negro poverty and humiliation in their manifold forms have substantially been accomplished. Demonstrations may be limited in the future, but contrary to some belief, they will not be abandoned. Demonstrations educate the onlooker as well as the participant, and education requires repetition. That is one reason why they have not outlived their usefulness. Furthermore, it would be false optimism to expect ready compliance to the new law everywhere. The Negro's weapon of non-violent direct action is his only serviceable tool against injustice. He may be willing to sheath that sword but he has learned the wisdom of keeping it sharp.

Yet new times call for new policies. Negro leadership, long attuned to agitation, must now perfect the art of organization. The movement needs stable and responsible institutions in the communities to utilize the new strength of Negroes in altering social customs. In their furious combat to level walls of segregation and discrimination, Negroes gave primary emphasis to their deprivation of dignity and personality. Having gained a measure of success they are now revealed to be clothed, by comparison with other Americans, in rags. They are housed in decaying ghettoes and provided with a ghetto education to eke out a ghetto life. Thus, they are automatically enlisted in the war on poverty as the most eligible combatants. Only when they are in full possession of their civil rights everywhere, and afforded equal economic opportunity, will the haunting race question finally be laid to rest.

What are the key guides to the future? It would not be over-optimistic to eliminate one of the vain hopes of the segregationists—the white backlash. It had a certain reality in 1964, but far less than the segregationists needed. For the most part it was powered by petulance rather than principle. Therefore, when the American people saw before them a clear choice between a future of progress with racial justice or stagnation with ancient privilege, they voted in landslide proportions for justice. President Johnson made a creative contribution by declining to mute this issue in the campaign.

The election of President Johnson, whatever else it might have been, was also an alliance of Negro and white for common interests. Perceptive Negro leadership understands that each of the major accomplishments in 1964 was the product of Negro militancy *on a level that could mobilize and maintain white support*. Negroes acting alone and in a hostile posture toward all whites will do nothing more than demonstrate that their conditions of life are unendurable, and that they are unbearably angry. But this has already been widely dramatized. On the other hand, whites who insist upon exclusively determining the time schedule of change will also fail, however wise and generous they feel themselves to be. A genuine Negro-white unity is the tactical foundation upon which past and future progress depends.

The rapid acceleration of change in race relations in the nation is occurring within the larger transformation of our political and economic structure. The South is already a split region, fissured politically and economically as cleanly as the Mississippi River divides its banks. Negroes by themselves did not fragment the South; they facilitated a process that the changing economy of the nation began. The old rural South, essentially poor and retarded, had to industrialize as agricultural regions contracted under the impact of heightened soil productivity. The exodus from Southern farms coincided with the influx of industry seeking the natural resources and cheaper labor market of the area.

Negroes were drawn off the farms into urban service and into limited, semi-skilled occupations. Though many migrated North, most remained in the South. Just as they had not been content to erode with the old plantations, they were not disposed to take a permanent place as industrial untouchables. The ferment of revolutionary change by the backward and dispossessed peoples of the whole world inspired them to struggle. In some areas, economic and social change enabled them to advance against an opposition that was still formidable but of a different quality than that of the past. The new South, with its local needs and with an eye to its national image, could not adhere to the brutal, terroristic overseer psychology of bygone days. For these reasons Atlanta, Savannah and some cities of Florida are markedly different from the underdeveloped belts of Mississippi, Louisiana and Alabama.

In the next period, Negroes are likely to find new white Southern allies of even greater importance among the rural and urban poor. It is an irony of American history that Negroes have been oppressed and subjected to discrimination by many whose economic circumstances were scarcely better than their own. The social advantages which softened the economic disabilities of Southern poor whites are now beginning to lose some of their attractions as these whites realize what material benefits are escaping them. The section of the Civil Rights Act of 1964 which withholds federal aid when it is used discriminatorily in federally assisted programs has revolutionary implications. It ties the interests of whites who desperately need relief from their impoverishment to the Negro who has the same needs. The barriers of segregation are splintering under the strain of economic deprivation which cuts across caste lines. To climb the economic ladder, Negro and white will have to steady it together, or both will fall.

This is already occurring among many who have run for office in different areas of the South. The faces were the same as of old, but looking closely, one could see that some of the features had changed. Especially, the language had changed: "Negro," not "darky"; "the law of the land," not "States' rights"; the "new prosperity and affluence," not the "old Southern traditions." These new phrases may be uttered with many private agonies, but their commitments are public.

Space does not permit a sufficient discussion of the President's program, nor is it yet adequately elaborated. But without wishing to diminish the high respect which the President earned from the civil rights movement, one aspect of his program should be studied, if only because of the emphasis he has given it. The President's concept of consensus must be subject to thoughtful and critical examination. The New York Times in a perceptive editorial on December 20 asked if Mr. Johnson really means to be a "consensus President." It pointed out that such were Coolidge and Eisenhower, who "served the needs of the day but not of decades to come. They preside over periods of rest and consolidation. They lead no probes into the future and break no fresh ground." The *Times* then added, "A President who wants to get things done has to be a fighter, has to spend the valuable coin of his own popularity, has to jar the existing consensus. . . . No major program gets going unless someone is willing to wage an active and often fierce struggle in its behalf."

The *Times* is undeniably correct. The fluidity and instability of American public opinion on questions of social change is very marked. There would have been no civil rights progress, nor a nuclear test-ban treaty, without resolute Presidential leadership. The issues which must be decided are momentous. The contest is not tranquil and relaxed. The search for a consensus will tend to become a quest for the least common denominator of change. In an atmosphere devoid of urgency the American people can easily be stupefied into accepting slow reform, which in practice would be inadequate reform. "Let Justice roll down like waters in a mighty stream," said the Prophet Amos. He was seeking not consensus but the cleansing action of revolutionary change. America has made progress toward freedom, but measured against the goal the road ahead is still long and hard. This could be the worst possible moment for slowing down.

A consensus orientation is understandably attractive to a political leader. His task is measurably easier if he is merely to give shape to widely accepted programs. He becomes a technician rather than an innovator. Past Presidents have often sought such a function. President Kennedy promised in his campaign an executive order banning discrimination in housing. This substantial progressive step, he declared, required only "a stroke of the pen." Nevertheless, he delayed execution of the order long after his election on the ground that he awaited a "national consensus." President Roosevelt, facing the holocaust of an economic crisis in the early thirties, attempted to base himself on a consensus with the N.R.A.; and generations earlier, Abraham Lincoln temporized and hesitated through years of civil war, seeking a consensus before issuing the Emancipation Proclamation.

In the end, however, none of these Presidents fashioned the program which was to mark him as historically great by patiently awaiting a consensus. Instead, each was propelled into action by a mass movement which did not necessarily reflect an overwhelming majority. What the movement lacked in support was less significant than the fact that it had championed the key issue of the hour. President Kennedy was forced by Birmingham and the tumultuous actions it stimulated to offer to Congress the Civil Rights Bill. Roosevelt was impelled by labor, farmers and small-businessmen to commit the government in revolutionary depth to social welfare as a constituent stimulus to the economy. Lincoln signed the Emancipation

Proclamation under the pressure of war needs. *The overwhelming national consensus followed their acts; it did not precede them.*

The contemporary civil rights movement must serve President Johnson in the same fashion. It must select from the multitude of issues those principal creative reforms which will have broad transforming power to affect the whole movement of society. Behind these goals it must then tirelessly organize widespread struggle. The specific selection of the correct and appropriate programs requires considerable discussion and is beyond the purview of this study. A few guidelines are, however, immediately evident.

One point of central importance for this period is that the distribution of Negroes geographically makes a single national tactical program impractical. During the Civil War, Frederick Douglass perceived the difference in problems of Negroes in the North and in the South. He championed emancipation, aside from its moral imperatives, because its impact would transform the South. For the North, his principal demand was integration of Negroes into the Union Army.

Similarly today, the Negro of the South requires in the first place the opportunity to exercise elementary rights and to be shielded from terror and oppression by reliable, alert government protection. He should not have to stake his life, his home or his security merely to enjoy the right to vote. On the other hand, in the North, he already has many basic rights and a fair measure of state protection. There, his quest is toward a more significant participation in government, and the restructuring of his economic life to end ghetto existence.

Very different tactics will be required to achieve these disparate goals. Many of the mistakes made by Northern movements may be traced to the application of tactics that work in Birmingham but produce no results in Northern ghettoes. Demonstrations in the streets of the South reveal the cruel fascism underlacing the social order there. No such result attends a similar effort in the North. However, rent strikes, school boycotts, electoral alliances summon substantial support from Negroes, and dramatize the specific grievances peculiar to those communities.

With the maturation of the civil rights movement, growing out of the struggles of 1963 and 1964, new tactical devices will emerge. The most important single imperative is that we continue moving forward with the indomitable spirit of those two turbulent years. It is worth recalling the admonition of Napoleon (he was thinking of conquest, but what he said was true also of constructive movements): "In order to have good soldiers, a nation must always be at war."

~ 1980 ~

Notes on the House of Bondage

James Baldwin

James Baldwin's first piece for a national magazine was a review, "Maxim Gorky as Artist," in *The Nation* (April 12, 1947). Thereafter, Baldwin published a series of landmark books, including *Go Tell It On the Mountain* (1953), *Notes of a Native Son* (1955), and *The Fire Next Time* (1963). He was a member of the magazine's editorial board from 1978 until his death in 1987. In this piece, Baldwin sheds light on the state of America by surveying the dispiriting array of candidates for the 1980 Presidential race.

November 1, 1980 ~ Gabriel's trumpet is a complex metaphor. Poor Gabriel is not only responsible for *when we dead awaken*—heavy enough—but he must also blow that trumpet *to wake the children sleeping*.

The children are always ours, every single one of them, all over the globe; and I am beginning to suspect that whoever is incapable of recognizing this may be incapable of morality. Or, I am saying, in other words, that we, the elders, are the only models children have. What we see in the children is what they have seen in us—or, more accurately perhaps, what they *see* in us.

I, too, find that a rather chilling formulation, but I can find no way around it. How am I, for example, to explain to any of my tribe of nieces and nephews and great-nieces and great-nephews how it happens that in a nation so boastfully autonomous as the United States we are reduced to the present Presidential candidates? I certainly do not want them to believe that Carter or Reagan—*or* Anderson—are the best people this country can produce. That despair would force me onto the road taken by the late, Guyana-based Jim Jones. But there they are, the pea-nut farmer and the third-rate, failed, ex–Warner Brothers contract player, both as sturdy and winning as Wheaties, and as well equipped to run the world as I am to run a post office.

There they are. And there is, also, the question, *Who* you *going to vote for, Uncle Jimmy?*

It can be said, of course—and let me say it before you do—that I am speaking as a black American. My testimony can, therefore, be dismissed out of hand by reason of my understandable (thank you) but quite unreasonable bitterness.

Well, I have had my bitter moments, certainly, days and ways, but I do not think that I can usefully be described as a bitter man. I would not be trying to write this if I were, for the bitter do not, mainly, speak: they, suddenly and quite unpredictably, act. The bitter can be masters, too, at telling you what you want to hear because they *know* what you want to hear. And how do they know that?

Well, some of them know it because they must raise their children and bring them to a place, somehow, where the American guile and cowardice cannot destroy them. No black citizen (!) of what is left of Harlem supposes that either Carter, or Reagan, or Anderson has any concern for them at all, except as voters—that is, to put it brutally, except as instruments, or dupes—and, while one hates to say that the black citizens are right, one certainly cannot say that they are wrong.

One has merely to look up and down the streets of Harlem; walk through the streets and into what is left of the houses; consider the meaning of this willed, inhuman and criminal devastation, and look into the faces of the children. *Who* you *going to vote for, Uncle Jimmy?*

John Brown, I have sometimes been known to say, but that flippant rage is, of course, no answer.

But, if we're to change our children's lives and help them to liberate themselves from the jails and hovels—the mortal danger—in which our countrymen have placed us, the vote does not appear to be the answer, either. It has certainly not been the answer until now.

Here one finds oneself on treacherous ground indeed. I am, legally anyway, an adult, a somewhat battered survivor of this hard place, and have never expected my power to vote to have any effect whatever on my life, and it hasn't. On the other hand, I have been active in voter registration drives in the South because the acquisition of the vote, there and then, and even if only for local aims, was too crucial and profound a necessity even to be argued. Nor can it be denied that the sheer tenacity of the black people in the South, their grace under pressure (to put it far too mildly) and the simple fact of their presence in the voting booth profoundly challenged, if it did not expose, the obscene Southern mythology.

Thus, though there is certainly no New South yet, the old one has no future, and neither does the "old" North. The situation of the black American is a direct (and deliberate) result of the collusion between the North and South and the Federal Government. A black man in this country does not live under a two-party system but a four-party system. There is the Republican Party in the South, and there is the Republican Party in the

North; there is the Democratic Party in the North and the Democratic Party in the South. These entities are Tweedledum and Tweedledee as concerns the ways they have been able, historically, to manipulate the black presence, the black need. At the same time, both parties were (are) protected from the deepest urgencies of black need by the stance of the Federal Government, which could (can) always justify both parties, and itself, by use of the doctrine of "States' rights."

In the South, then, the Republican Party was the *nigra's* friend, and, in the North, it was the Democrats who lovingly dried our tears. But, however liberal Northern Democrats might seem to be, nothing was allowed to menace the party unity—certainly not niggers—with the result that the presumed or potential power of the black vote in the North was canceled out by the smirk on the faces of the candidates in the South. The party had won—was in—and we were out. What it came to was that, as long as blacks in the South could not vote, blacks in the North could have nothing to vote for. A very clever trap, which only now, and largely because of the black vote in the South, may be beginning to be sprung.

The American institutions are all bankrupt in that they are unable to deal with the present—resembling nothing so much as Lot's wife. When Americans look out on the world, they see nothing but dark and menacing strangers who appear to have no sense of rhythm at all, nor any respect or affection for white people; and white Americans really do not know what to make of all this, except to increase the defense budget.

This panic-stricken saber rattling is also for the benefit of the domestic darker brother. The real impulse of the bulk of the American people toward their former slave is lethal: if he cannot be used, he should be made to disappear. When the American people, Nixon's no-longer-silent majority, revile the Haitian, Cuban, Turk, Palestinian, Iranian, they are really cursing the nigger, and the nigger had better know it.

The vote does not work for a black American the way it works for a white one, for the despairingly obvious reason that whites, in general, are welcomed to America, and blacks, in general, are not. Yet, risking a seeming contradiction, one may go further and point out that America's egalitarian image is very important to American self-esteem. Therefore, blacks from the West Indies, say, or Africa, who arrive with no social or political quarrels with the United States, who have already been formed by the island, or village community, and who bring their mercantile skills with them, are likely to fare much better here than Sambo does—for a brief and melancholy season. Since the entire country is bizarre beyond belief, the black immigrant does not quarrel with its customs, considering that these customs have nothing to do with him. He sticks to his kith and kin, and saves his pennies, and is the apple of the white American eye, for he proves that the Yankee-Puritan virtues are all that one needs to prosper in this brave new world.

This euphoria lasts, at most, a generation. In my youth, the West Indians, who assured American blacks that *they*, the West Indians, had never been slaves, ran their stores, saved their pennies, went bankrupt and, as a community, disappeared—or, rather, became a part of the larger black community. Later on, the Puerto Ricans were hurled into this fire and, after the brief, melancholy and somewhat violent season, we began to compare notes, and share languages, and now here come, among others, the Haitians, and the beginning of the end of the doctrine of divide-and-rule, at least as concerns the dark people of the West.

The white person of the West is quite another matter. His presence in America, in spite of vile attacks on "the foreign-born," poses no real problem. Within a generation, at most two, he is at home in his new country and climbing that ladder. If there is trouble in the Irish, Italian or Polish ward, say, the trouble can be contained and eliminated because the demands of these white people do not threaten the fabric of American society. This proved to be true during even the bloodiest of the worker-industrial clashes: white workers opted for being white first and workers second—and, in the land of the free and the home of the brave, who said that they had to remain workers? It was easy enough to turn the white worker against the black worker by threatening to put the black man in the white man's job, at a lower salary. Once the white worker had fallen into this trap, the rest was child's play: the black was locked out of the unions, the unions and big business got in bed together and, whenever there was trouble in the ghetto, white America, as one man, cried, *What does the Negro want?* Billy clubs, tear gas, guns and cold-blooded murder imposed a sullen order, and a grateful Republic went back to sleep.

This has been the American pattern for all of the years that I have been on earth, and, of course, for generations before that, and I have absolutely no reason to believe that this leopard has changed his spots. Nixon was elected, after all, received his "mandate," by means of the Omnibus Crime Bill and the "Safe Streets Act" ("safe streets" meaning *keep the nigger in his place*) and his crony, the late and much lamented Gov. Nelson Rockefeller, who was responsible for the Attica slaughter, passed the Hitlerian "No-knock Stop and Frisk Law," which brought every black person in New York a little closer to the madhouse and the grave. The Nixon career was stopped by Watergate, God be praised, and by the intervention of a black man, thank our ancestors; but Attorney General John Mitchell had already corralled several thousands of us, black and white, in a ballpark.

The United States is full of ballparks. My black vote, which has not yet purchased my autonomy, may yet, if I choose to use it, keep me out of the ballpark long enough to figure out some other move. Or for the children to make a move. Or for aid to come from somewhere. My vote will probably not get me a job or a home or help me through school or prevent another Vietnam or a third World War, but it may keep me here long enough for me to see, and use, the turning of the tide—for the tide has got to turn. And, since I am not the only black man to think this way, if Carter is re-elected, it will be by means of the black vote, and it will not be a vote for Carter. It will be a coldly calculated risk, a means of buying time. Perhaps only black people realize this, but we are dying, here, out of all proportion to our numbers, and with no respect to age, dying in the streets, in the madhouse, in the tenement, on the roof, in jail and in the Army. This is not by chance, and it is not an act of God. It is a result of the action of the American institutions, all of which are racist: it is revelatory of the real and helpless impulse of most white Americans toward black people.

Therefore, in a couple of days, blacks may be using the vote to outwit the Final Solution. Yes. The Final Solution. No black person can afford to forget that the history of this country is genocidal, from where the buffalo once roamed to where our ancestors were slaughtered (from New Orleans to New York, from Birmingham to Boston) and to the Caribbean to Hiroshima and Nagasaki to Saigon. Oh, yes, let freedom ring.

Why are you voting for Carter, Uncle Jimmy? Well, don't, first of all, take this as an endorsement. It's meant to be a hard look at the options, which, however, may no longer exist by the time you read this, may no longer exist as I write.

I lived in California when Ronald Reagan was Governor, and that was a very ugly time—the time of the Black Panther harassment, the beginning (and the end) of the Soledad Brothers, the persecution, and trial, of Angela Davis. That, all that, and much more, but what I really found unspeakable about the man was his contempt, his brutal contempt, for the poor.

Perhaps because he is a Southerner, there lives in Carter still—I think—an ability to be tormented. This does not necessarily mean much, so many people preferring torment to action, or responsibility, and it is, furthermore, a very real question (for some; some would say that it's not a question at all) as to how much of Carter belongs to Carter. But if he can still be tormented, he can be made to pause—the machinery can be made to pause—and we will have to find a way to use that pause.

It is terror that informs the American political and social scene—the terror of leaving the house of bondage. It isn't a terror of seeing *black* people leave the house of bondage, for white people think that they *know* that this cannot *really* happen, not even to Leontyne Price, or Muhammad Ali, who are, after all, "exceptions," with white blood, and mortal. No, white people had a much better time in the house of bondage than we did, and God bless their souls, they're going to miss it—all that adulation, adoration, ease, with nothing to do but fornicate, kill Indians, breed slaves and make money. Oh, there were rough times, too, as *Shane*, *True Grit* and *Rocky* inform us, but the rules of the game were clear, and the rewards demanded nothing more complex than stamina. God was a businessman, like all "real" Americans, and understood that "business was business." The American innocence was unassailable, fixed forever, for it was not a crime to kill a black or a red or a yellow man. On the contrary, it might be, and was most often so considered, a duty. It was not a crime to rape a black or red or yellow woman—it was sport; besides, *niggers ought to be glad we pump some white blood into their kids every once in a while.* The lowest white man was more exalted than the most articulate or eminent black: an exceedingly useful article of faith both for the owners of the Southern fields and the bosses in the Northern sweatshops, who worked this exalted creature past senility to death.

Thus, what the house of bondage accomplished for what we will call the classic white American was the destruction of his moral sense, except in relation to whites. But it also destroyed his sense of reality and, therefore, his sense of white people had to be as compulsively one-dimensional as his vision of blacks. The result is that white Americans have been one another's jailers for generations, and the attempt at individual maturity is the loneliest and rarest of the American endeavors. (This may also be why a "boyish" look is a very decided advantage in the American political and social arena.)

Well, the planet is destroying the American fantasies; which does not give the Americans the right to destroy the planet. I don't know if it is possible to speak coherently concerning what my disturbed countrymen want, but I hazard that, although the Americans are certainly capable of precipitating Armageddon, their most desperate desire is to make time stand still. If time stands still, it can neither judge nor accuse nor exact payment; and, indeed, this is precisely the bargain the black presence was expected to strike in the white Republic. It is why the black face had always to be a happy face.

Recently, the only two black shows on Broadway were minstrel shows. There was a marvelous current between the blacks on the stage and the blacks in the audience. Both knew why the white audience was there, and to watch white audiences being reassured by a minstrel show can be grotesque and sorrowful beyond belief. But the minstrel show is really no different from the TV screen which celebrates, night after night and year after year and decade after decade, the slaughter of the Native American and pretends (in spite of *Roots*, which demands a separate assessment) that the black enslavement never occurred.

Well. It did occur, and *is* occurring all up and down America, as I write, and is crossing borders and being exported to various "underdeveloped" portions of the globe. But this endeavor cannot succeed, with force or without it, because the center of the earth has shifted. The British Prime Minister, for example, is a grotesque anachronism, and the world is not holding its breath waiting to see what will happen in England; England's future will be determined by what is happening in the world.

I am speaking of the breakup—the end—of the so-overextended Western empire. I am thinking of the black and nonwhite peoples who are shattering, redefining and recreating history—making all things new—simply by declaring their presence, by delivering their testimony. The empire never intended that this testimony should be heard, but, *if I hold my peace, the very stones will cry out.*

One can speak, then, of the fall of an empire at that moment when, though all of the paraphernalia of power remain intact and visible and seem to function, neither the citizen-subject within the gates nor the indescribable hordes outside it believe in the morality or the reality of the kingdom anymore—when no one, any longer, anywhere, aspires to the empire's standards.

This is the charged, the dangerous, moment, when everything must be re-examined, must be made new; when nothing at all can be taken for granted. One looks again at the word "famine." At this hour of the world's history, famine must be considered a man-made phenomenon and one looks at who is starving. There is nothing even faintly ridiculous, or unfair, in these apprehensions, which are produced by nothing less than Western history. Our former guides and masters are among the most ruthless creatures in mankind's history, slaughtering and starving one another to death long before they discovered the blacks. If the British were willing to starve Ireland to death—which they did, in order to protect the profits of British merchants—why would the West be reluctant to starve Africa out of existence? Especially since the generation facing famine now is precisely that generation that will begin the real and final liberation of Africa from Europe. It is, in any case, perfectly clear that the earth's populations can be fed if—or, rather, when—we alter our priorities. We can irrigate deserts and feed the entire earth for the price we are paying to build bombs that we will be able to use, in any event, only once; after which whoever is left will have to begin doing what I am suggesting now. It would be nice if we could, for once, make it easy on ourselves.

The elders, especially at this moment of our black-white history, are indispensable to the young, and vice versa. It is of the utmost importance, for example, that I, the elder, do not allow myself to be put on the defensive. The young, no matter how loud they get, have no real desire to humiliate their elders and, if and when they succeed in doing so, are lonely, crushed and miserable, as only the young can be.

Someone my age, for example, may be pleased and proud that Carter has blacks in his Cabinet. A younger person may wonder just what their function is in such a Cabinet. They will be keenly aware, too, that blacks called upon to represent the Republic are, very often, thereby prohibited from representing blacks. A man my age, schooled in adversity and skilled in compromise, may choose not to force the issue of defense spending versus the bleak and criminal misery of the black *and* white populations here, but a younger man may say, out loud, that he will not fight for a country that has *never* fought for him and, further, that the myth and menace of global war are nothing more and nothing less than a coward's means of distracting attention from the real crimes and concerns of this Republic. And they may have to visit him in prison, or suffer with him there—no matter. The irreducible miracle is that we have sustained each other a very long time, and come a long, long way together. We have come to the end of a language and are now about the business of forging a new one. For we have survived, children, the very last white country the world will ever see.

~ 1991 ~

On Patriotism

Jesse Jackson

For its 125th anniversary issue, *The Nation* asked writers and activists to explain their interpretation of patriotism. Jesse Jackson contributed the following thoughts.

July 15/22, 1991 ~ One afternoon in Greenville, South Carolina, when I was 9 years old, my father was raking leaves. The man came outside to offer us a drink of water, and when he left I asked, Why does that man speak differently from us? "He's German," said my father, and he stopped and leaned on his rake. "He's German. I fought in Europe so they could have freedom. I'm proud to be a veteran of that war." His eyes clouded over. "But now he's here, and he can vote, and I cannot. I helped free his people, now I'm raking his leaves."

It is a paradox of the human spirit that even after such brutal oppression and disregard for human rights, we are still so patriotic and love our country so much. It is our land; we cultivated it and helped to build it. But it is not our government. Indeed, fighting for a better government is the patriotic thing to do.

America at its best guarantees opportunity, and so fighting to expand the horizons of oppressed people is an act of patriotism. Yet too often, those who dare expand our nation's democracy and make it true to its principles are victims of naked aggression, aggression led not by street fighters but by the White House, Congress and the courts. The founding writers of the Constitution envisioned a nation in which people of African descent were three-fifths human, in which their own mothers and daughters and sisters had no right to vote, in which Native Americans had no right to live. Thomas Jefferson expressed the American dilemma when he wrote:

> For in a warm climate, no man will labour for himself who can make another labour for him. This is so true, that of the proprietors of slaves a very small proportion indeed are ever seen to labour. And can the liberties of a nation be thought secure when we have removed their only firm basis, a conviction in the minds of the people that these liberties are of the gift of God? That they

are not to be violated but with his wrath? Indeed I tremble for my country when I reflect that God is just. . . .

Through patriotism we have made America better. We have gained the right to vote. Women and African-Americans have changed the course and character of the nation. And my father's faith in his country has been sustained in the lifetime commitment of his family to make America better. Yet those who have fought for the highest and best principles of our country, the true patriots, have been vilified and crucified. The true patriots invariably disturb the comfortable and comfort the disturbed, and are persecuted in their lifetimes even as their accomplishments are applauded after their deaths.

Today, politicians are proud to pronounce that we have abolished slavery. But in its time, slavery was the political center, and abolitionists were punished for their moral strength. Today, politicians hold up the gains of women. Yet in its time, denial of the vote to women was the political center; the women's suffrage movement sought the moral center, and was punished for its patriotism. Those who fight for civil rights, open housing, environmental laws, peace and international cooperation, and veterans of domestic wars—the real patriots—receive no parades.

We must never relinquish our sense of justice for a false sense of national pride. "My country right or wrong" is neither moral nor intelligent. Patriotism is support for the highest ideals of the nation, not for whoever happens to be in the White House. As citizens we must continue to fight for justice and equality so that we might make a better nation and a better world. We must give credence to our invitation: "Give me your tired, your poor, your huddled masses yearning to breathe free," for the character of our nation is rooted in the affirmation of these ideals for all of our people.

~ 1993 ~

Where's the Revolution?

Barbara Smith

Barbara Smith is the editor of *Home Girls: A Feminist Anthology*
and the publisher of Kitchen Table: Women of Color Press.
This essay was written for *The Nation*'s special issue "A Queer
Nation."

July 5, 1993 ~ Revolution seems like a largely irrelevant concept to the gay
movement of the nineties. The liberation politics of the earlier era, which
relied upon radical grass-roots strategies to eradicate oppression, have been
largely replaced by an assimilationist "civil rights" agenda. The most visible
elements of the movement have put their faith almost exclusively in electoral and legislative initiatives, bolstered by mainstream media coverage, to
alleviate *discrimination*. When the word "radical" is used at all, it means con-
frontational, "in your face" tactics, not strategic organizing aimed at the
roots of oppression.

Unlike the early lesbian and gay movement, which had both ideological
and practical links to the left, black activism and feminism, today's "queer"
politicos seem to operate in a historical and ideological vacuum. "Queer"
activists focus on "queer" issues, and racism, sexual oppression and economic exploitation do not qualify, despite the fact that the majority of "queers"
are people of color, female or working class. When other oppressions or
movements are cited, it's to build a parallel case for the validity of lesbian
and gay rights or to expedite alliances with mainstream political organizations. Building unified, ongoing coalitions that challenge the system and
ultimately prepare a way for revolutionary change simply isn't what "queer"
activists have in mind.

When lesbians and gay men of color urge the gay leadership to make
connections between heterosexism and issues like police brutality, racial
violence, homelessness, reproductive freedom and violence against women
and children, the standard dismissive response is, "Those are not our
issues." At a time when the gay movement is under unprecedented public
scrutiny, lesbians and gay men of color and others committed to antiracist
organizing are asking: Does the gay and lesbian movement want to create a

just society for everyone? Or does it only want to eradicate the last little glitch that makes life difficult for privileged (white male) queers?

The April 25 March on Washington, despite its historical importance, offers some unsettling answers. Two comments that I've heard repeatedly since the march is that it seemed more like a parade than a political demonstration and that the overall image of the hundreds of thousands of participants was overwhelmingly Middle American, that is, white and conventional. The identifiably queer—the drag queens, leather people, radical faeries, dykes on bikes, etc.—were definitely in the minority, as were people of color, who will never be Middle American no matter what kind of drag we put on or take off.

A friend from Boston commented that the weekend in Washington felt like being in a "blizzard." I knew what she meant. Despite the fact that large numbers of lesbians and gay men of color were present (perhaps even more than at the 1987 march), our impact upon the proceedings did not feel nearly as strong as it did six years ago. The bureaucratic nineties concept of "diversity," with its superficial goal of assuring that all the colors in the crayon box are visible, was very much the strategy of the day. Filling slots with people of color or women does not necessarily affect the politics of a movement if our participation does not change the agenda, that is, if we are not actually permitted to lead.

I had had my own doubts about attending the April march. Although I went to the first march in 1979 and was one of the eight major speakers at the 1987 march, I didn't make up my mind to go to this one until a few weeks before it happened. It felt painful to be so alienated from the gay movement that I wasn't even sure I wanted to be there; my feelings of being an outsider had been growing for some time.

I remember receiving a piece of fundraising direct mail from the magazine *Outlook* in 1988 with the phrase "tacky but we'll take it" written next to the lowest potential contribution of $25. Since $25 is a lot more than I can give at any one time to the groups I support, I decided I might as well send my $5 somewhere else. In 1990 I read Queer Nation's manifesto, "I Hate Straights," in *Outweek* and wrote a letter to the editor suggesting that if queers of color followed its political lead, we would soon be issuing a statement titled, "I Hate Whiteys," including white queers of European origin. Since that time I've heard very little public criticism of the narrowness of lesbian and gay nationalism. No one would guess from recent stories about wealthy and "powerful" white lesbians on TV and in slick magazines that women earn 69 cents on the dollar compared with men and that black women earn even less.

These examples are directly connected to assumptions about race and class privilege. In fact, it's gay white men's racial, gender and class privileges, as well as the vast numbers of them who identify with the system rather than distrust it, that have made the politics of the current gay movement so different from those of other identity-based movements for social and political change. In the seventies, progressive movements—especially feminism—positively influenced and inspired lesbians' and gays' vision of struggle. Since the eighties, as AIDS has helped to raise consciousness about gay issues in some quarters of the establishment, and as some battles against homophobia have been won, the movement has positioned itself more and more within the mainstream political arena. Clinton's courting of the gay vote (at the same time as he did everything possible to distance himself from the African-American community) has also been a crucial factor in convincing the national gay and lesbian leadership that a place at the ruling class's table is just what they've been waiting for. Of course, the people left out of this new gay political equation of mainstream acceptance, power and wealth are lesbians and gay men of color.

It was talking to radical lesbians and gay men that finally made me decide to go to the April 25 march. Earlier in the month, I attended an extraordinary conference on the lesbian and gay left in Delray Beach, Florida. The planners had made a genuine commitment to racial and gender parity; 70 percent of the participants were people of color and 70 percent were women. They were also committed to supporting the leadership of people of color and lesbians—especially lesbians of color—which is almost never done outside of our own autonomous groupings. The conference felt like a homecoming. I got to spend time with people I'd worked with twenty years before in Boston as well as with younger activists from across the country.

What made the weekend so successful, aside from the humor, gossip, caring and hot discussions about sex and politics, was the huge relief I felt at not being expected to cut off parts of myself that are as integral to who I am as my sexual orientation as the price for participating in lesbian and gay organizing. Whatever concerns were raised, discussions were never silenced by the remark, "But that's not our issue." Women and men, people of color and whites, all agreed that there desperately needs to be a visible alternative to the cut-and-dried, business-as-usual agenda of the gay political mainstream. Their energy and vision, as well as the astuteness and tenacity of radical lesbians and gays I encounter all over the country, convince me that a different way is possible.

If the gay movement ultimately wants to make a real difference, as opposed to settling for handouts, it must consider creating a multi-issue revolutionary agenda. This is not about political correctness, it's about winning. As black lesbian poet and warrior Audre Lorde insisted, "The master's tools will never dismantle the master's house." Gay *rights* are not enough for me, and I doubt that they're enough for most of us. Frankly, I want the same thing now that I did thirty years ago when I joined the civil rights movement, and twenty years ago when I joined the women's movement, came out and felt more alive that I ever dreamed possible: freedom.

~ 1994 ~

Conversations about *Brown:* Among Moses' Bridge-Builders

Patricia J. Williams

Nation contributing editor Patricia J. Williams visited Linda Brown Thompson, the little girl on whose behalf Oliver Brown sued in 1954, and her family in Kansas. Also present were her mother, Mrs. Leola Brown Montgomery, the middle daughter, Terry Brown Tyler; and Cheryl Brown Henderson, the youngest daughter. The resulting conversation appeared in *The Nation*'s special issue commemorating the 40th anniversary of the *Brown v. Topeka Board of Education* decision.

May 23, 1994 ~ "Our family came to Kansas for the railroad in 1923," said Mrs. Leola Brown patiently, apparently quite used to cutting through the exuberant excesses of questions with no borders, never mind answers. "A lot of the early African-American and Hispanic residents of Topeka came for employment purposes. The headquarters of the Santa Fe railroad were here. There were decent wages and you could be part of a union and have job security, those sorts of things."

"When did you join the N.A.A.C.P.?" I pressed, longing for detail about what, at odd moments, I caught myself thinking of as "our" story. "Were there any significant events in your life that precipitated your involvement in the case against the school board?"

"We joined for no specific incident. It was in 1948 or '49, something like that. There was nothing specific. It was everything. We were discriminated against in all phases of life. We couldn't go to the restaurants or the shows, or if we did, we had to sit in a certain place, we had to go through a certain door to get there. . . . " she trailed off. "It wasn't only about the schools, you see, it was about all of the things that were against us, all the rejection and neglect, all the things we could not do here."

As Mrs. Leola Brown spoke, describing conditions that affected millions of blacks as well as her family, I understood why her daughters were so insistent on my not making this story into an exceptional one. It was a story that couldn't, shouldn't be made into private property; it was an exemplary story, but far from unique.

My family too joined the N.A.A.C.P. not because of a great event but because of all the ordinary daily grinding little events that made life hard in the aggregate. I knew the back of the bus stories, the peanut gallery stories, the baggage car stories, the having to go to the bathroom in the woods stories—the myriad, mundane, nearly invisible yet monumentally important constraints that circumscribed blacks, and not only in the South.

My father, who grew up in Savannah, Georgia, during the 1920s and '30s, remembers not only the inconveniences but the dangers of being black under Jim Crow. "You had to be careful of white people; you got out of the way, or you'd get hurt, immediately. If you saw a white person coming, you got off the sidewalk. Don't make too much noise. Know which side of the street to walk on. You were always conscious of the difference. The big conversation in all 'colored' homes was just that, color. It affected everybody."

"That's exactly why *Brown* is indeed 'our' story," advised a friend of mine who, being fifteen or so years older than I, was old enough to have worked for N.A.A.C.P. causes and gone on enough marches to have worn out many pairs of shoes. "The civil rights movement was all about ordinary people who weren't necessarily on the road to Damascus. If some lent their names, others lent their backs, or their expertise or their lives. It was life-threatening work after all, so nobody did it to get their name up in lights; you did it because there was no alternative. Neither fame nor anonymity existed as issues per se—that's come later, as the country seems to have sorted out who it's going to remember and what it will forget. It was about group survival. You were always thinking about what would make it better for the children."

I pressed the Browns about this centrality of segregation in people's lives. Segregation affected most aspects of daily life, they explained, but they noted that the situation in Kansas was not exactly like what was going on in many Southern states. The neighborhood in which the Browns lived, for example, was fully integrated at the time the suit was initiated, and unlike many children even today, Linda Brown, in the wake of the case, was able to finish her education at integrated schools. The Browns describe most of the neighborhoods in Topeka as having been pretty stable over time—although the Browns' old neighborhood and the all-white school that was the object of the suit no longer exist. "The highway has come through." Although Topeka did undergo some of the divisive and segregating effects of urban renewal programs, the Browns say Topeka did not undergo major upheavals during the 1960s, as did most Northern cities where white flight changed "urban centers" into "inner cities" overnight.

Kansas is indeed unique in history, but it is not alone in the peculiarity of its contradictory attitudes about race. Perhaps part of the difficulty in reviewing the years since *Brown* with anything like a hopeful countenance is that we as a nation have continued to underestimate the complicated and multiple forms of prejudice at work in the United States. Segregation did not necessarily bar all forms of racial mixing; its odd, layered hierarchies of racial attitude were substantially more complicated than that. My grandfather, for example, was a doctor who owned many of the houses in the neighborhood where he lived. "Dad's tenants were white, Irish," says my father. "But I never even thought about where they went to school. We all lived kind of mixed up, but the whole system made you think so separately that to this day I don't know where they went to school." There is an old story that speaks to the profundity of these invisible norms: Three men in the 1930s South set out to go fishing in a small boat. They spent the morning in perfectly congenial and lazy conversation. At lunchtime, they all opened their lunch buckets and proceeded to eat, but not before the two white men put an oar across the middle of the boat, dividing them from their black companion.

The continuing struggle for racial justice is tied up with the degree to which segregation and the outright denial of black humanity have been *naturalized* in our civilization. An aunt of mine who is very light-skinned tells of a white woman in her office who had just moved from Mississippi to Massachusetts. "The North is much more racist than the South," she confided to my aunt. "They don't give you any credit at all for having white blood."

Have you been disappointed by the years since 1954? I asked Mrs. Leola Brown Montgomery. Of course, she said. And then added, "But I don't think that anybody anticipated the country's response. The attorneys, the parents, we didn't really understand the insidious nature of discrimination and to what lengths people would go to not share educational resources: leaving neighborhoods en masse because African-American children could now go to the school in your neighborhood. Not offering the same kinds of programs, or offering a lesser educational program in the same school—I don't think anybody anticipated what we've ended up with. . . . But we're currently still in the midst of the country's response, in my opinion."

"Growing up," says my father, "we thought we knew exactly what integration meant. We would all go to school together; it meant the city would spend the same money on you that it did on the white students. We blacks wouldn't be in some cold isolated school that overlooked the railroad yards; we wouldn't have to get the cast-off, ragged books. We didn't think about the inevitability of a fight about whose version of the Civil War would be taught in that utopic integrated classroom."

For all the biblical imagery summoned to inspire the will to go on with the civil rights struggle in this country, if the waters have parted at any given moment, perhaps it has been more attributable to all those thousands of busy bridge-builders working hard to keep Moses' back covered—just people, just working and thinking about how it could be different, dreaming big, yet surprised most by the smallest increments, the little things that stun with the realization of the profundity of what has not yet been thought about.

My father muses: "It's funny . . . we talked about race all the time, yet at the same time you never really thought about *how* it could be different. But after *Brown* I remember it dawning on me that I *could* have gone to the University of Georgia. And people began to talk to you a little differently." The white doctor who treated my family in Boston, where I grew up, "used to treat us in such a completely offhand way. But after *Brown*, he wanted to discuss it with us, he asked questions, what I thought. He wanted my opinion and I suddenly realized that no white person had ever asked what I thought about anything."

Perhaps as people like my father and the doctor have permitted those conversations to become more and more straightforward, the pain of it all, the discomfort, has been accompanied by the shutting down, the mishearing, the turning away from the euphoria of *Brown*. "It has become unexpectedly, but not unpredictably, hard. The same thing will probably have to happen in South Africa," sighs my father.

When Frederick Douglass described his own escape from slavery as a "theft" of "this head" and "these arms" and "these legs," he employed the master's language of property to create the unforgettable paradox of the "owned" erupting into the category of a speaking subject whose "freedom" simultaneously and inextricably marked him as a "thief." That this disruption of the bounds of normative imagining is variously perceived as dangerous as well as liberatory is a tension that has distinguished racial politics in America from the Civil War to this day. Perhaps the legacy of *Brown* is as much tied up with this sense of national imagination as with the pure fact of its legal victory; it sparkled in our heads, it fired our vision of what was possible. Legally it set in motion battles over inclusion, participation and reallocation of resources that are very far from resolved. But in a larger sense it committed us to a conversation about race in which all of us must join—particularly in view of a new rising Global Right.

The fact that this conversation has fallen on hard times is no reason to abandon what has been accomplished. The word games by which the civil rights movement has been stymied—in which "inner city" and "underclass" and "suspect profile" are racial code words, in which "integration" means "assimilation as white," in which black culture means "tribalism," in which affirmative action has been made out to be the exact equivalent of quota systems that discriminated against Jews—these are all dimensions of the enormous snarl this nation has been unraveling, in waves of euphoria and despair, since the Emancipation Proclamation.

We remain charged with the task of getting beyond the stage of halting encounters filled with the superficial temptations of those "my maid says blacks are happy" or "whites are devils" moments. If we could press on to an accounting of the devastating legacy of slavery that lives on as a social crisis that needs generations more of us working to repair—if we could just get to the enormity of that unhappy acknowledgment, then that alone might be the paradoxical source of a genuinely revivifying, rather than a false, optimism.

The most eloquent summary of both the simplicity and the complexity of that common task remains W.E.B. Du Bois's essay "On Being Crazy":

> After the theatre, I sought the hotel where I had sent my baggage. The clerk scowled.
>
> "What do you want?" he said.
>
> Rest, I said.
>
> "This is a white hotel," he said.
>
> I looked around. Such a color scheme requires a great deal of cleaning, I said, but I don't know that I object.
>
> "We object," said he.
>
> Then why, I began, but he interrupted.
>
> "We don't keep niggers," he said, "we don't want social equality."
>
> Neither do I, I replied gently, I want a bed.

INDEX